PRAYERS THAT AVAIL MUCH®

For Women

James 5:16

Prayers That Avail Much®
For Women

James 5:16

by
Germaine Copeland

And this is the confidence that we have in him, that, if we ask any thing according to his will, he heareth us: and if we know that he hear us, whatsoever we ask, we know that we have the petitions that we desired of him.

1 John 5:14,15

Harrison House
Tulsa, Oklahoma

Calligraphy by Victoria Lane

Prayers That Avail Much is a registered trademark of
Word Ministries, Inc., a Georgia corporation.

05 04 03 02   10 9 8 7 6 5 4 3 2 1

Prayers That Avail Much for Women®
ISBN 1-57794-489-5
(formerly ISBN 1-57794-127-6)
Copyright © 2002 by Germaine Copeland
(formerly copyright © 1997)
38 Sloan Street
Roswell, Georgia 30075

Published by Harrison House, Inc.
P. O. Box 35035
Tulsa, Oklahoma 74153

PRESENTED TO

TERRi

BY

TED + Nancy
-$

DATE

July 19, 2002

OCCASION

Because we Love You!

Contents

Part II: Prayers for Relationships

Part III: Prayers for Career

Part IV: Prayers for Ministry

A Word to Women

Dear Friend,

Welcome to the *Prayers That Avail Much Family Series.* There are many issues facing today's woman, and demands for your time may seem overwhelming. *Prayers That Avail Much for Women* is a compilation of prayers from our existing books that we believe will be helpful in scheduling and keeping your prayer appointments with God. These prayers will inspire and motivate you to achieve spiritual growth and emotional wholeness.

Developing an effectual prayer life and consistently reading the Bible enables you to become more intimately acquainted with God. You learn to recognize and understand His nature, and appreciate the value He has placed on you. The God Who created woman is the Lord Who gives the word [of power]. He calls women to bear and publish the good news, and we are a great host (Psalm 68:11 AMP).

In the beginning when God created all things He said, "Now we will make humans, and they will be like us. We will let them rule the fish, the birds, and all other living creatures." So God created humans to be like himself; he made men and women (Genesis 1:26-27 CEV).

What were God's intentions when He designed woman? Did God give equal power and ability to both the woman and man? Does God allow women to minister in the church? What do you believe about the woman in Proverbs 31? After attempting to be this woman, I concluded that she is a composite of God's woman describing various gifts and talents deposited within the makeup of individuals. God created you a distinctive person, and I want to encourage you to find the answers to these questions. The Holy Spirit is the One Who will guide you into all Truth — the reality of who you are.

It takes valuable time to answer these questions. The church and society at one time were very specific in defining "WOMAN" according to her roles. In the environment where I grew up it was understood that the woman would stay in her place at home and in the church. Was this "place" God's place for her? Who decided that she was too emotional to make decisions, and that her ideas and opinions were invalid? God declares that you are a capable, intelligent, and virtuous woman more precious than jewels, and your value is far above rubies or pearls (Proverbs 31:10). Our Lord Jesus honored women, defended women, and valued women. Jesus brought redemption to everyone — both men and women. He delivered those in bondage to sin, forgave them, and restored them to wholeness.

After many years of fighting to break out of the mold designed for me by others, I came to know the Creator as my Heavenly Father. It would require much studying, praying, and emotional healing before I quit fighting to be the "me" God created. I could not make this happen — I was not able to change me — there seemed to be no escape from my prisons of guilt, shame, fear, and intimidation. God provided a way of escape where there seemed to be *no* way. My escape was in the Person of Jesus Christ. He is the Way, the Truth, and the Life. In the presence of God I learned that I am free to make choices. My "today" is a result of choices I made yesterday. Spiritual growth and emotional wholeness allowed me to assume responsibility for my choices.

In *Prayers That Avail Much for Women* we have provided you a starting place. Find a quiet, peaceful space, and set aside time, preferably, at the beginning of your day to commune with God. Begin by addressing Him as "Our Father." Acknowledge His Sovereignty asking Him to hallow His Name in your personality, and in all your roles and activities. Ask for His will to be done, for His Kingdom to come in all your decisions and encounters. Make your petitions known to Him forgiving others as freely as He has forgiven you. Affirm the Lordship of Jesus and submit to the constant ministry of transformation by the Holy Spirit.

Part 1 includes prayers for personal needs. It is God's desire that you know His will for your life. In God's divine providence there is healing for crippled and damaged emotions. He delivered you out of the authority of darkness and translated you into the Kingdom of His dear Son. Old thought patterns are replaced with new and the metamorphosis from "victim" to "victor" becomes a reality. You are more than a conqueror through Him that loves you. Learning to live victoriously is a process that takes time. We have to train our senses to know right from wrong. You will overcome personal fears — fear of failure, of being alone, or of having to prove yourself to others. You can look in the mirror and approve of the "you" God created. He gives you the grace to come out of the snare of the enemy. You will no longer fear the opinions of man.

You were born for such a time as this. Do you know who you are? Do you know why you were born? What is your mission in life? Do you know your strengths? It seems that most of us know our weaknesses. Are you able to glory in your weaknesses allowing the power of God to prevail? Knowing the answers to these questions will give you direction and empower you to make wise decisions. As you assume responsibility for your decisions, you will reap the rewards.

Relationships are important to us, and we have a special section of prayers that will prepare you for developing healthy relationships with God, with family, and with others. I meet many single women who are looking for a man to complete themselves. Concentrate on becoming the woman that God created you to be, and you will not have to expose yourself to ungodly, unholy alliances that result in guilt and condemnation.

The battered woman feels trapped, and wonders if she will ever find a way out. Some continue living with abusive men thinking that things will change — they will get better. Others have given up hope of the situation ever changing, and go from one storm to another, grateful for the lulls. The addictions and behaviors of the significant other controls their thoughts and behavior.

Prayer prepares you to practice tough love, make godly decisions and necessary changes.

Often, women are angry with God for His failure to intervene in situations that they actualized by their unwise choices. They seem eager to hold onto unhealthy relationships believing that they can change the other person, willing to stay no matter how great the emotional cost to them and their children. What kind of values and standards are we teaching our children?

Women living in abusive relationships, often believe they are "right" and want God to correct the husband or significant other. On occasion a caller to our ministry becomes angry when we dare minister that God called her to peace, not to accept her husband's infidelities and endure abuses. There are several things we share with them.

- God does not require you to live with abuse. Once when the crowd wanted to throw Jesus off a cliff, He turned and walked away. Change begins with you, and change brings change. God has instructed us to put on the new nature created in Christ Jesus — give up old behaviors, change our attitudes and thoughts to agree with

His will. When we enable others to sin against us we become a partner in their sin and its penalties.

- Do not isolate yourself believing that no one else has ever suffered as you. The Word says that our sufferings are common to man. Attend a local church were you can receive godly counseling and guidance. Today, many churches have support groups where you will encounter those who understand your distress from personal experience. As they share the comfort they have received, you are comforted and encouraged.

- We pray with them asking God to give them the courage to take the action necessary to protect themselves and their children.

When everyone we have trusted betrays us, it is difficult to trust a God we cannot see. "Oh, for grace to trust Him more." Feelings of insecurity often control a woman's decisions to stay in an unhealthy, dangerous situation. One emotionally crippled woman shared that it was worth being abused to feel loved during peaceful times. She was able to walk away when she embraced the truth that Jesus loves me! Do not give up who you are created to be, or compromise your convictions to win the praise and approval of others.

Live truly, speak truly, and deal truly in all the affairs of life. Make your ear attentive to skillful and godly Wisdom. Wisdom that comes from heaven is...whole-hearted and straightforward and sincere (James 3:17 LB). Walk in truth developing the fruit of the spirit, and follow the Holy Spirit in every area of your life. Choose your priorities. "Seek (aim at and strive after) first of all His kingdom and His righteousness (His way of doing and being right)..." (Matthew 6:33 AMP).

Hide God's Word in your heart. Know His teachings. They are true life and good health for you. Carefully guard your thoughts because they are the source of true life. Never tell lies or be deceitful in what you say (Proverbs 2:2-4 CEV). When you maintain godly integrity, you will walk in righteousness, in love, and in obedience to the Word of God.

Many women are controlled by the fear of never marrying, of being alone, of never having children — and the list goes on. Satan takes advantage of these fears and works his schemes to defeat and destroy women. Satan has hated women since Genesis 3:15. God said to

him, "From now on you and the woman will be
enemies, as will your offspring and hers. You will strike
his heel, but he will crush your head." Jesus, our Savior,
defeated him, stripped him of his power and authority.
Today, we are the enforcers of the triumphant victory of
our Lord Jesus Christ. It is time for each individual
woman to arise, determine her worth and set high standards according to the will and purpose of God.

Unmarried women look at their married sisters, and
cry, "You don't understand!" Many married women
would gladly exchange their marriage problems for
those of a single person. Some believe a woman is
incomplete and made to feel "less than" worthy as a
person without a mate. In some churches a single
woman is never allowed to hold a leadership role
because she is "unbalanced" without a spouse. How
tragic that the church has forfeited its opportunity to
train a powerful leader, and sacrificed valuable talents for
man-made doctrines.

If single and married women could have an open
forum, both would discover that wholeness comes out of
a personal relationship with Christ Jesus our Lord. You
are complete in Him. More than one married woman
has said, "I can't find myself. I don't know who I am.

Why do I feel unfulfilled? What is wrong with me? I feel so fragmented." Many times they blame the spouse. The chastisement needful to obtain our peace, emotional healing, and wellbeing was upon Jesus (Isaiah 53:5). When Jesus came and dwelt among us He revealed Jehovah as a loving Father. As you develop an intimate relationship with Him, you will learn to appreciate and to love yourself, and then, you can receive love and risk loving others.

You will find prayers to strengthen you whether you are single or married, a stay-at home Mother, or a career person. Before beginning the day, prepare yourself by spending time in prayer and meditation. Yes, I am in ministry, and I love my work. Each day before I go to the office, I allow time to pray, meditate, and read God's Word and other helpful, inspiring materials for personal growth. When my children were home I had to rise early to have the necessary quiet time with my Father in prayer and Bible study. Jesus is made unto us wisdom, righteousness, sanctification, and redemption (1 Corinthians 1:30).

Prayer is conversation with our Heavenly Father. Take time to talk with Him and listen for His quiet, gentle voice. He knows your present circumstances and your future, and has already provided exactly what you need for the day. Collect your thoughts and prepare to take care of the daily activities. May God receive glory and honor as we go about our daily routines. I pray that others will come to know our Father Who is in heaven just because we have been in prayer with Jesus.

My prayer is that you will find strength, comfort, courage, and fortitude as you pray according to God's Word. Grow in grace and the knowledge of our Lord and Savior Jesus Christ, ever learning, ever growing, and ever achieving. Faith comes by hearing, and hearing by the Word. When you hear yourself pray you will discover that you truly believe. God is a rewarder of those who believe that He is, and that He is a rewarder of those who diligently seek Him.

Oh, what manner of love has the Father bestowed upon you that He would call you His daughter! You are a daugher of the Most High God. He equips you to overcome obstacles and to succeed in every area of your life. You are God's woman!

Loving in Jesus' Name,
Germaine Copeland
Your Sister in Christ

Personal Confessions

Jesus is Lord over my spirit, my soul, and my body (Phil. 2:9-11).

Jesus has been made unto me wisdom, righteousness, sanctification, and redemption. I can do all things through Christ Who strengthens me (1 Cor. 1:30, Phil. 4:13).

The Lord is my Shepherd. I do not want. My God supplies all my needs according to His riches in glory in Christ Jesus (Ps. 23, Phil. 4:19).

I do not fret or have anxiety about anything. I do not have a care (Phil. 4:6, 1 Pet. 5:6,7).

I am the Body of Christ. I am redeemed from the curse, because Jesus bore my sicknesses and carried my diseases in His own body. By His stripes I am healed. I forbid any sickness or disease to operate in my body. Every organ, every tissue of my body functions in the perfection in which God created it to function. I honor God and bring glory to Him in my body (Gal. 3:13, Matt. 8:17, 1 Pet. 2:24, 1 Cor. 6:20).

I have the mind of Christ and hold the thoughts, feelings, and purposes of His heart (1 Cor. 2:16).

I am a believer and not a doubter. I hold fast to my confession of faith. I decide to walk by faith and practice faith. My faith comes by hearing and hearing by the Word of God. Jesus is the Author and the Developer of my faith (Heb. 4:14, Heb. 11:6, Rom. 10:17, Heb. 12:2).

The love of God has been shed abroad in my heart by the Holy Spirit and His love abides in me richly. I keep myself in the Kingdom of light, in love, in the Word, and the wicked one touches me not (Rom. 5:5, 1 John 4:16, 1 John 5:18).

I tread upon serpents and scorpions and over all the power of the enemy. I take my shield of faith and quench his every fiery dart. Greater is He Who is in me than he who is in the world (Ps. 91:13, Eph. 6:16, 1 John 4:4).

I am delivered from this present evil world. I am seated with Christ in heavenly places. I reside in the Kingdom of God's dear Son. The law of the Spirit of life in Christ Jesus has made me free from the law of sin and death (Gal. 1:4, Eph. 2:6, Col. 1:13, Rom. 8:2).

I fear not for God has given me a spirit of power, of love, and of a sound mind. God is on my side (2 Tim. 1:7, Rom. 8:31).

I hear the voice of the Good Shepherd. I hear my Father's voice, and the voice of a stranger I will not follow. I roll my works upon the Lord. I commit and trust them wholly to Him. He will cause my thoughts to become agreeable to His will, and so shall my plans be established and succeed (John 10:27, Prov. 16:3).

I am a world overcomer because I am born of God. I represent the Father and Jesus well. I am a useful member in the Body of Christ. I am His workmanship recreated in Christ Jesus. My Father God is all the while effectually at work in me both to will and do His good pleasure (1 John 5:4,5, Eph. 2:10, Phil. 2:13).

I let the Word dwell in me richly. He Who began a good work in me will continue until the day of Christ (Col. 3:16, Phil. 1:6).

Part I

PRAYERS FOR
PERSONAL NEEDS

To Receive Jesus as Savior and Lord

Father, it is written in Your Word that if I confess with my mouth that Jesus is Lord and believe in my heart that You have raised Him from the dead, I shall be saved. Therefore, Father, I confess that Jesus is my Lord. I make Him Lord of my life right now. I believe in my heart that You raised Jesus from the dead. I renounce my past life with Satan and close the door to any of his devices.

I thank You for forgiving me of all my sin. Jesus is my Lord, and I am a new creation. Old things have passed away. Now all things become new in Jesus' name. Amen.

Scripture References

John 3:16	John 14:6
John 6:37	Romans 10:9,10
John 10:10b	Romans 10:13
Romans 3:23	Ephesians 2:1-10
2 Corinthians 5:19	2 Corinthians 5:17
John 16:8,9	John 1:12
Romans 5:8	2 Corinthians 5:21

To Glorify God

In view of God's mercy, I offer my body as a living
sacrifice, holy and pleasing to God — this is my spiritual act of worship. It is [not in my own strength] for it
is You, Lord, Who is all the while effectually at work in
me — energizing and creating in me the power and
desire — both to will and work for Your good pleasure
and satisfaction and delight.

Father, I will not draw back or shrink in fear, for
then Your soul would have no delight or pleasure in me.
I was bought for a price — purchased with a precious-
ness and paid for, made Your very own. So, then, I
honor You, Lord, and bring glory to You in my body.

I called on You in the day of trouble; You delivered me, and I shall honor and glorify you. I rejoice
because You delivered me and drew me to Yourself
out of the control and dominion of darkness *(obscu-
rity)* and transferred me into the Kingdom of the Son
of Your love. I will confess and praise You, O Lord my
God, with my whole (united) heart; and I will glorify
Your name for evermore.

As a bond servant of Jesus Christ, I receive and develop the talents which have been given me, for I would have You say of me, "Well done, you upright (honorable, admirable) and faithful servant!" I make use of the gifts (faculties, talents, qualities) according to the grace given me. I let my light so shine before men that they may see my moral excellence and my praiseworthy, noble, and good deeds, and recognize and honor and praise and glorify my Father Who is in heaven.

In the name of Jesus, I allow my life to lovingly express truth in all things — speaking truly, dealing truly, living truly. Whatever I do — no matter what it is — in word or deed, I do everything in the name of the Lord Jesus and in [dependence upon] His Person, giving praise to God the Father through Him. Whatever may be my task, I work at it heartily (from the soul), as [something done] for the Lord and not for men. To God the Father be all glory and honor and praise. Amen.

Scripture References (AMP)

Romans 12:1	Matthew 25:21
Philippians 2:13	Romans 12:6
Hebrews 10:38b	Matthew 5:16
1 Corinthians 6:20	Ephesians 4:15
Psalm 50:15	Colossians 3:17
Colossians 1:13	Colossians 3:23
Psalm 86:12	

Knowing God's Will

Father, in Jesus' name, I thank You that You are instructing me in the way which I should go and that You are guiding me with Your eye. I thank You for Your guidance and leading concerning Your will, Your plan, and Your purpose for my life. I do hear the voice of the Good Shepherd, for I know You and follow You. You lead me in the paths of righteousness for Your name's sake.

Thank You, Father, that my path is growing brighter and brighter until it reaches the full light of day. As I follow You, Lord, I believe my path is becoming clearer each day.

Thank You, Father, that Jesus was made unto me wisdom. Confusion is not a part of my life. I am not confused about Your will for my life. I trust in You and lean not unto my own understanding. As I acknowledge You in all my ways, You are directing my paths. I believe that as I trust in You completely, You will show me the path of life. Amen.

Scripture References

Psalm 32:8

John 10:3,4

Psalm 23:3

Proverbs 4:18

Ephesians 5:19

1 Corinthians 1:30

1 Corinthians 14:33

Proverbs 3:5,6

Psalm 16:11

Godly Wisdom in the Affairs of Life

Father, You said if anyone lacks wisdom, let him ask
of You, Who giveth to all men liberally, and upbraideth
not; and it shall be given him. Therefore, I ask in faith,
nothing wavering, to be filled with the knowledge of
Your will in all wisdom and spiritual understanding.
Today I incline my ear unto wisdom, and apply my
heart to understanding so that I might receive that
which has been freely given unto me.

In the name of Jesus, I receive skill and godly
wisdom and instruction. I discern and comprehend the
words of understanding and insight. I receive instruction
in wise dealing and the discipline of wise thoughtful-
ness, righteousness, justice, and integrity. Prudence,
knowledge, discretion, and discernment are given to me.
I increase in knowledge. As a person of understanding, I
acquire skill and attain to sound counsels [so that I may
be able to steer my course rightly].

Wisdom will keep, defend, and protect me; I love
her and she guards me. I prize Wisdom highly and exalt
her; she will bring me to honor because I embrace her.

She gives to my head a wreath of gracefulness; a crown
of beauty and glory will she deliver to me. Length of
days is in her right hand, and in her left hand are riches
and honor.

Jesus has been made unto me wisdom, and in Him
are all the treasures of [divine] wisdom, [of comprehensive insight into the ways and purposes of God], and [all
the riches of spiritual] knowledge and enlightenment are
stored up and lie hidden. God has hidden away sound
and godly wisdom and stored it up for me, for I am the
righteousness of God in Christ Jesus.

Therefore, I will walk in paths of uprightness.
When I walk, my steps shall not be hampered — my
path will be clear and open; and when I run I shall not
stumble. I take fast hold of instruction, and do not let
her go; I guard her, for she is my life. I let my eyes look
right on [with fixed purpose], and my gaze is straight
before me. I consider well the path of my feet, and I let
all my ways be established and ordered aright.

Father, in the name of Jesus, I look carefully to how
I walk! I live purposefully and worthily and accurately,
not as unwise and witless, but as a wise — sensible,

intelligent person; making the very most of my time —
buying up every opportunity. Amen.

Scripture References

James 1:5,6a	1 Corinthians 1:30
Colossians 1:9b	Colossians 2:3 AMP
Proverbs 2:2	Proverbs 2:7 AMP
Proverbs 1:2-5 AMP	2 Corinthians 5:21
Proverbs 4:6,8,9 AMP	Proverbs 4:11-13,25,26 AMP
Proverbs 3:16 AMP	Ephesians 5:15,16 AMP

Conquering the Thought Life

In the name of Jesus, I take authority over my thought life. Even though I walk (live) in the flesh, I am not carrying on my warfare according to the flesh and using mere human weapons. For the weapons of my warfare are not physical (weapons of flesh and blood), but they are mighty before God for the overthrow and destruction of strongholds. I refute arguments and theories and reasonings and every proud and lofty thing that sets itself up against the (true) knowledge of God; and I lead every thought and purpose away captive into the obedience of Christ, the Messiah, the Anointed One.

With my soul I will bless the Lord with every thought and purpose in life. My mind will not wander out of the presence of God. My life shall glorify the Father — *spirit, soul, and body.* I take no account of the evil done to me — I pay no attention to a suffered wrong. It holds no place in my thought life. I am ever ready to believe the best of every person. I gird up the loins of my mind, and I set my mind and keep it set on what is above — the higher things — not on the things that are on the earth.

Whatever is true, whatever is worthy of reverence and is honorable and seemly, whatever is just, whatever is pure, whatever is lovely and lovable, whatever is kind and winsome and gracious, if there is any virtue and excellence, if there is anything worthy of praise, I will think on and weigh and take account of these things — I will fix my mind on them.

I have the mind of Christ, the Messiah, and do hold the thoughts (feelings and purposes) of His heart. In the name of Jesus, I will practice what I have learned and received and heard and seen in Christ, and model my way of living on it, and the God of peace — of untroubled, undisturbed wellbeing — will be with me.

In Jesus' name, amen.

Scripture References (AMP)

2 Corinthians 10:3-5

Psalm 103:1

1 Corinthians 6:20

1 Corinthians 13:5b,7a

1 Peter 1:13

Colossians 3:2

Philippians 4:8

1 Corinthians 2:16

Philippians 4:9

Walking in Humility

Father, I clothe myself with humility [as the garb of a servant, so that its covering cannot possibly be stripped from me]. I renounce pride and arrogance. Father, You give grace to the humble. Therefore I humble myself under Your mighty hand, that in due time You may exalt me.

In the name of Jesus, I cast the whole of my care [all my anxieties, all my worries, all my concerns for my future, once and for all] on You, for You care for me affectionately and care about me watchfully. I expect a life of victory and awesome deeds because my actions are done on behalf of a spirit humbly submitted to Your truth and righteousness.

Father, in the name of Jesus, I refuse to be wise in my own eyes; but I choose to fear You and shun evil. This will bring health to my body and nourishment to my bones.

Father, I humble myself and submit to Your Word that speaks...exposes, sifts, analyzes, and judges the very thoughts and purposes of my heart. I test my own actions, so that I might have appropriate self-esteem, without comparing myself to anyone else. The security of Your guidance will allow me to carry my own load with energy and confidence.

I listen carefully and hear what is being said to me. I incline my ear to wisdom and apply my heart to understanding and insight. Humility and fear of You bring wealth and honor and life.

Father, I hide Your Word in my heart that I might not sin against You. As one of Your chosen people, holy and dearly loved, I clothe myself with compassion, kindness, humility, gentleness, and patience. I bear with others and forgive whatever grievances I may have against anyone. I forgive as You forgave me. And over all these virtues I put on love, which binds them all together in perfect unity. I let the peace of Christ rule in my heart, and I am thankful for Your grace and the power of the Holy Spirit.

Father, may Your will be done on earth in my life as it is in heaven.

In Jesus' name, amen.

Scripture References

1 Peter 5:5-7 AMP

Proverbs 3:7,8 NIV

Hebrews 4:12 AMP

Galatians 6:4,5 NIV

Proverbs 2:2 NIV

Proverbs 22:4 NIV

Psalm 119:11

Colossians 3:12-15 NIV

Matthew 6:10 NIV

To Watch What You Say

Father, today, I make a commitment to You in the name of Jesus. I turn from idle words and foolishly talking things that are contrary to my true desire to myself and toward others. Your Word says that the tongue defiles; that the tongue sets on fire the course of nature; that the tongue is set on fire of hell.

In the name of Jesus, I submit to godly wisdom that I might learn to control my tongue. I am determined that hell will not set my tongue on fire. I renounce, reject, and repent of every word that has ever proceeded out of my mouth against You, God, and Your operation. I cancel its power and dedicate my mouth to speak excellent and right things. My mouth shall utter truth.

Because I am the righteousness of God in Christ Jesus, I set the course of my life for obedience, for abundance, for wisdom, for health, and for joy. Set a guard over my mouth, O Lord; keep watch over the door of my lips. Then the words of my mouth and my deeds shall show forth Your righteousness and Your salvation all of my days. I purpose to guard my mouth and my tongue that I might keep myself from calamity.

Father, Your words are top priority to me. They are spirit and life. I let the Word dwell in me richly in all wisdom. The ability of God is released within me by the words of my mouth and by the Word of God. I speak Your Words out of my mouth. They are alive in me. You are alive and working in me. So, I can boldly say that my words are words of faith, words of power, words of love, and words of life. They produce good things in my life and in the lives of others. Because I choose Your Words for my lips, I choose Your will for my life, in Jesus' name. Amen.

Scripture References

Ephesians 5:4	Proverbs 21:23
2 Timothy 2:16	Ephesians 4:27
James 3:6	James 1:6
Proverbs 8:6,7	John 6:63
2 Corinthians 5:21	Colossians 3:16
Proverbs 4:23	Philemon 6

To Live Free From Worry

Father, I thank You that I have been delivered from the power of darkness and translated into the Kingdom of Your dear Son. *I commit to live free from worry in the name of Jesus,* for the law of the Spirit of life in Christ Jesus has made me *free* from the law of sin and death.

I humble myself under Your mighty hand that in due time You may exalt me. I cast the whole of my cares *(name them)* — all my anxieties, all my worries, all my concerns — once and for all on You. You care for me affectionately and care about me watchfully. You sustain me. You will never allow the consistently righteous to be moved — made to slip, fall, or fail!

Father, I delight myself in You, and You perfect that which concerns me.

I cast down imaginations (reasonings) and every high thing that exalts itself against the knowledge of You, and I bring into captivity every thought to the obedience of Christ. I lay aside every weight and the sin of worry which does try so easily to beset me. I run with patience the race that is set before me, looking unto Jesus, the author and finisher of my faith.

I thank You, Father, that You are able to keep that which I have committed unto You. I think on (fix my mind on) those things that are true, honest, just, pure, lovely, of good report, virtuous, and deserving of praise. I will not let my heart be troubled. I abide in Your Word, and Your Word abides in me. Therefore, Father, I do *not* forget what manner of person I am. I look into the perfect law of liberty and continue therein, being *not* a forgetful hearer, but a *doer of the Word* and thus blessed in my doing!

Thank You, Father. *I am carefree.* I walk in that peace which passes all understanding in Jesus' name! Amen.

Scripture References

Colossians 1:13	Hebrews 12:1,2
Romans 8:2	2 Timothy 1:12
1 Peter 5:6,7 AMP	Philippians 4:8
Psalm 55:22	John 14:1
Psalm 138:8	James 1:22-25
2 Corinthians 10:5	Philippians 4:6

Pleading the Blood of Jesus

I.
Morning Prayer [1]

Father, I come in the name of Jesus to plead His blood on my life and on all that belongs to me, and on all that over which You have made me a steward.

I plead the blood of Jesus on the portals of my mind, my body (the temple of the Holy Spirit), my emotions, and my will. I believe that I am protected by the blood of the Lamb that gives me access to the Holy of Holies.

I plead the blood on my children, my grandchildren, and their children, and on all those whom You have given me in this life.

Lord, You have said that the life of the flesh is in the blood. Thank You for this blood that has cleansed me from sin, and sealed the New Covenant of which I am a partaker.

In Jesus' name, amen.

---

[1] Based on a prayer written by Joyce Meyer in *The Word, the Name and the Blood* (Tulsa: Harrison House, 1995).

Scripture References

Exodus 12:7,13	Leviticus 17:11
1 Corinthians 6:19	1 John 1:7
Hebrews 9:6-14	Hebrews 13:20 AMP

II.
Evening Prayer [2]

Father, as I lie down to sleep, I plead the blood of Jesus upon my life — within me, around me, and between me and all evil and the author of evil.

In Jesus' name, amen.

---

[2] Based on a prayer written by Mrs. C. Nuzum as recorded by Billye Brim in *The Blood and the Glory* (Tulsa: Harrison House, 1995).

Breaking the Curse of Abuse

Introduction

**Christ redeemed us from the curse of the law
by becoming a curse for us, for it is written:
"Cursed is everyone who is hung on a tree."**

Galatians 3:13 NIV

On a Sunday morning after I had taught a lesson titled "Healing for the Emotionally Wounded," a young man wanted to speak with me. I listened intently as he told me that he had just been released from jail and was now on probation for physically abusing his family. His wife had filed for divorce, and he was living alone. It was not easy for him to confess his sin to me, and I was impressed by his humble attitude.

He said, "I am glad that this message is being given in the church, and the abused can receive ministry. Is there anywhere that the abuser can go to receive spiritual help?"

He shared with me that he was attending a support group for abusers. He desired to commit to a church where he could receive forgiveness and acceptance. He knew that any lasting change would have to be from the inside out by the Spirit. I prayed with him, but it would be three years before I could write a prayer for the abuser.

As I read, studied, and sought the Lord, I discovered that the abuser is usually a person who has been abused. Often, the problem is a generational curse that has been in the family of the abuser for as far back as anyone can remember. Many times the abuser declares that he will never treat his wife and children as he has been treated, but in spite of his resolve he finds himself reacting in the same violent manner.

The generational curse is reversed as the abuser is willing to allow God to remove the character flaws that have held him in bondage.

If you are an abuser, I encourage you to pray this prayer for yourself until it becomes a reality in your life. If you know someone who is an abuser, pray this as a prayer of intercession in the third person.

Prayer

I receive and confess that Jesus is my Lord, and I ask that Your will be done in my life.

Father, You have rescued me from the dominion of darkness and have brought me into the Kingdom of the Son of Your love. Once I was darkness, but now I am light in You; I walk as a child of light. The abuse is exposed and reproved by the light, it is made visible and clear; and where everything is visible and clear there is light.

Help me to grow in grace (undeserved favor, spiritual strength) and recognition and knowledge and understanding of my Lord and Savior, Jesus Christ, so that I may experience Your love and trust You to be a Father to me.

The history of my earthly family is filled with abusive behavior, much hatred, strife, and rage. The painful memory of past abuse *(verbal, emotional, physical, and/or sexual)* has caused me to be hostile and abusive to others.

I desire to be a doer of the Word, and not a hearer only. No matter which way I turn, I can't make myself do right. I want to, but I can't. When I want to do good, I don't; and when I try not to do wrong, I do it anyway. It seems that sin still has me in its evil grasp. This pain has caused me to hurt myself and others. In my mind I want to be Your willing servant, but instead I find myself still enslaved to sin.

I confess my sin of abuse, resentment, and hostility toward others, and I ask You to forgive me. You are faithful and just to forgive my sin and cleanse me from all unrighteousness. I am tired of reliving the past in my present life, perpetuating the generational curse of anger and abuse.

Jesus was made a curse for me; therefore, Lord, I put on Your whole armor that I may be able to successfully stand against all the strategies and the tricks of the devil. I thank You that the evil power of abuse is broken, overthrown, and cast down. I submit myself to You and resist the devil. The need to hurt others no longer controls me or my family.

In Jesus' name, amen.

Scripture References

Romans 10:9	Romans 7:18-25 TLB
Matthew 6:10	1 John 1:9
Colossians 1:13 AMP	Galatians 3:13
Ephesians 5:8,13 AMP	Ephesians 6:11,12 TLB
2 Peter 3:18 AMP	2 Corinthians 10:5
James 1:22	James 4:7

Healing From Abuse

Introduction

This prayer can be applied to any form of abuse —
physical, mental, emotional, or sexual. I wrote it after
reading T. D. Jakes' book, *Woman, Thou Art Loosed.*[4] By
praying it, I personally have experienced victory and
freedom — I am no longer a victim but an overcomer.

Prayer

Lord, You are my High Priest, and I ask You to
loose me from this "infirmity." The abuse I suffered
pronounced me guilty and condemned. I was bound —
in an emotional prison — crippled, and could in no wise
lift up myself. You have called me to Yourself, and I
have come.

The anointing that is upon You is present to bind
up and heal the brokenness and emotional wounds of
the past. You are the Truth that makes me free.

---

[1] (Shippensburg, PA: Treasure House, 1993).

Thank You, Lord, for guiding me through the steps to emotional wholeness. You have begun a good work in me, and You will perform it until the day of Christ Jesus.

Father, I desire to live according to the Spirit of life in Christ Jesus. This Spirit of life in Christ, like a strong wind, has magnificently cleared the air, freeing me from a fated lifetime of brutal tyranny at the hands of abuse.

Since I am now free, it is my desire to forget those things that lie behind and strain forward to what lies ahead. I press on toward the goal to win the [supreme and heavenly] prize to which You in Christ Jesus are calling me upward. The past will no longer control my thinking patterns or my behavior.

Praise be to You! I am a new creature in Christ Jesus. Old things have passed away; and, behold, all things have become new. I declare and decree that henceforth I will walk in newness of life.

Forgive me, Father, for self-hatred and self-condemnation. I am Your child. You sent Jesus that I might have life and have it more abundantly. Thank You for the blood of Jesus that makes me whole.

It is my desire to throw all spoiled virtue and cancerous evil into the garbage. In simple humility, I let my Gardener, You Lord, landscape me with the Word, making a salvation-garden of my life.

Father, by Your grace, I forgive my abuser/abusers and ask You to bring him/her/them to repentance.

In the name of Jesus I pray, amen.

Scripture References

Luke 13:11,12	Romans 6:4
John 14:6	1 John 3:1,2
John 8:32	John 10:10
Philippians 1:6	1 John 1:7
Romans 8:2 MESSAGE	James 1:21 MESSAGE
Philippians 3:13,14 AMP	Matthew 5:44
2 Corinthians 5:17	2 Peter 3:9

Letting Go of the Past

Father, I realize my helplessness in saving myself, and I glory in what Christ Jesus has done for me. I let go — put aside all past sources of my confidence — counting them worth less than nothing, in order that I may experience Christ and become one with Him.

Lord, I have received Your Son, and He has given me the authority (power, privilege, and right) to become Your child.

I unfold my past and put into proper perspective those things that are behind. I have been crucified with Christ, and I no longer live, but Christ lives in me. The life I live in the body, I live by faith in the Son of God, Who loved me and gave Himself for me. I trust in You, Lord, with all my heart and lean not on my own understanding. In all my ways I acknowledge You, and You will make my paths straight.

I want to know Christ and the power of His resurrection and the fellowship of sharing in His sufferings, becoming like Him in His death, and so, somehow, to attain to the resurrection from the dead. So, whatever it takes, I will be one who lives in the fresh newness of life of those who are alive from the dead.

I don't mean to say that I am perfect. I haven't learned all I should even yet, but I keep working toward that day when I will finally be all that Christ saved me for and wants me to be.

I am bringing all my energies to bear on this one thing: regardless of my past I look forward to what lies ahead. I strain to reach the end of the race and receive the prize for which You are calling me up to heaven because of what Christ Jesus did for me.

In His name I pray, amen.

Scripture References

Philippians 3:7-9 TLB

John 1:12 AMP

Psalm 32:5 AMP

Philippians 3:13

Galatians 2:20 NIV

Proverbs 3:5,6 NIV

Philippians 3:10,11 NIV

Romans 6:4

Philippians 3:12-14 TLB

Strength To Overcome Cares and Burdens

Why are you cast down, O my inner self? And why should you moan over me and be disquieted within me?

Father, You set Yourself against the proud and haughty, but give grace [continually] unto the humble. I submit myself therefore to You, God. In the name of Jesus, I resist the devil, and he will flee from me. I resist the cares of the world which try to pressure me daily. Except the Lord builds the house, they labor in vain who build it.

Jesus, I come to You, for I labor and am heavy laden and over burdened, and You cause me to rest — You will ease and relieve and refresh my soul.

I take Your Yoke upon me, and I learn of You; for You are gentle (meek) and humble (lowly) in heart, and I will find rest — relief, ease, and refreshment, and recreation, and blessed quiet — for my soul. For Your Yoke is wholesome *(easy)* — not harsh, hard, sharp, or pressing, but comfortable, gracious, and pleasant; and Your burden is light and easy to be borne.

I cast my burden on You, Lord, [releasing the weight of it] and You will sustain me; I thank You that

You will never allow me, the [consistently] righteous, to be moved — made to slip, fall, or fail.

In the name of Jesus, I withstand the devil. I am firm in my faith [against his onset] — rooted, established, strong, immovable, and determined. I cease from [the weariness and pain] of human labor; and am zealous and exert myself and strive diligently to enter into the rest [of God] — to know and experience it for myself.

Father, I thank You that Your presence goes with me, and that You give me rest. I am still and rest in You, Lord; I wait for You, and patiently stay myself upon You. I will not fret myself, nor shall I let my heart be troubled, neither shall I let it be afraid. I hope in You, God, and wait expectantly for You; for I shall yet praise You, for You are the help of my countenance, and my God.

In Jesus' name, amen.

Scripture References (AMP)

Psalm 42:11a	Hebrews 4:10b,11
James 4:6,7	Exodus 33:14
Psalm 127:1a	Psalm 37:7
Matthew 11:28-30	John 14:27b
Psalm 55:22	Psalm 42:11b
1 Peter 5:9a	

Healing for Damaged Emotions

Father, in the name of Jesus, I come to You with a feeling of shame and emotional hurt. I confess my transgressions to You [continually unfolding the past till all is told]. You are faithful and just to forgive me and cleanse me of all unrighteousness. You are my hiding place and You, Lord, preserve me from trouble. You surround me with songs and shouts of deliverance. I have chosen life and according to Your Word You saw me while I was being formed in my mother's womb and on the authority of Your Word I was wonderfully made. Now, I am Your handiwork, recreated in Christ Jesus.

Father, You have delivered me from the spirit of fear and I shall not be ashamed. Neither shall I be confounded and depressed. You gave me beauty for ashes, the oil of joy for mourning, and the garment of praise for the spirit of heaviness that I might be a tree of righteousness, the planting of the Lord, that You might be glorified. I speak out in psalms, hymns, and spiritual songs, offering praise with my voice and making melody with all my heart to the Lord. Just as David did in 1 Samuel 30:6, I encourage myself in the Lord.

I believe in God Who raised Jesus from the dead,
Who was betrayed and put to death because of my
misdeeds and was raised to secure my acquittal, absolv-
ing me from all guilt before God. Father, You anointed
Jesus and sent Him to bind up and heal my broken
heart, and liberate me from the shame of my youth and
the imperfections of my caretakers. In the name of
Jesus, I choose to forgive all those who have wronged
me in any way. You will not leave me without support as
I complete the forgiveness process. I take comfort and
am encouraged and confidently say, "The Lord is my
Helper; I will not be seized with alarm. What can man
do to me?"

My spirit is the candle of the Lord searching all the
innermost parts of my being and the Holy Spirit leads
me into all truth. When reality exposes shame and
emotional pain, I remember that the sufferings of this
present life are not worth being compared with the
glory that is about to be revealed to me and in me and
for me and conferred on me! The chastisement needful
to obtain my peace and wellbeing was upon Jesus, and
with the stripes that wounded Him I was healed and
made whole. As Your child, Father, I have a joyful and

confident hope of eternal salvation. This hope will never disappoint, delude, or shame me, for God's love has been poured out in my heart through the Holy Spirit Who has been given to me.

In His name I pray, amen.

Scripture References

Psalm 32:5-7 AMP	Romans 4:24,25
1 John 1:9	Isaiah 61:1
Deuteronomy 30:19	Mark 11:25
Psalm 139	Hebrews 13:5,6
Ephesians 2:10	Proverbs 20:27
2 Timothy 1:7	John 16:13
Isaiah 54:4	Romans 8:18
Isaiah 61:3	Isaiah 53:5b
Ephesians 5:19	Romans 5:3-5

Victory Over Pride

Father, Your Word says that You hate a proud look, that You resist the proud but give grace to the humble. I submit myself therefore to You, God. In the name of Jesus, I resist the devil, and he will flee from me. I renounce every manifestation of pride in my life as sin; I repent and turn from it.

As an act of faith, I clothe myself with humility and receive Your grace. I humble myself under Your mighty hand, Lord, that You may exalt me in due time. I refuse to exalt myself. I do not think of myself more highly than I ought; I do not have an exaggerated opinion of my own importance, but rate my ability with sober judgment, according to the degree of faith apportioned to me.

Proverbs 11:2 says, **When pride cometh, then cometh shame: but with the lowly is wisdom.** Father, I set myself to resist pride when it comes. My desire is to be counted among the lowly, so I take on the attitude of a servant.

Father, thank You that You dwell with him who is of a contrite and humble spirit. You revive the spirit of the humble and revive the heart of the contrite ones. Thank You that the reward of humility and the reverent and worshipful fear of the Lord is riches and honor and life.

In Jesus' name I pray, amen.

Scripture References

Proverbs 6:16

James 4:6,7

Proverbs 21:4

1 Peter 5:5,6

Romans 12:3 AMP

Proverbs 11:2

Matthew 23:11

Isaiah 57:15

Proverbs 22:4 AMP

Victory in a Healthy Lifestyle

Father, I am Your child, and Jesus is Lord over my spirit, soul, and body. I praise You because I am fearfully and wonderfully made. Your works are wonderful; I know that full well.

Lord, thank You for declaring Your plans for me — plans to prosper me and not to harm me, plans to give me hope and a future. I choose to renew my mind to Your plans for a healthy lifestyle. You have abounded toward me in all prudence and wisdom. Therefore, I give thought to my steps. Teach me knowledge and good judgment.

My body is for the Lord. So here is what I want to do with Your help, Father God. I choose to take my everyday, ordinary life — my sleeping, eating, going-to-work, and walking-around life — and place it before You as an offering. Embracing what You do for me is the best thing I can do for You.

Christ the Messiah will be magnified and will receive glory and praise in this body of mine and will be

boldly exalted in my person. Thank You, Father, in
Jesus' name! Hallelujah! Amen.

Scripture References

Psalm 139:14	Psalms 119:66
Jeremiah 29:11	Romans 12:1 MESSAGE
Proverbs 14:15	Philippians 1:20 AMP

Victory Over Fear

Father, when I am afraid, I will put my confidence in You. Yes, I will trust Your promises. And since I trust You, what can mere man do to me?

You have not given me a spirit of timidity, but of power and love and discipline (sound judgment). Therefore, I am not ashamed of the testimony of my Lord. I have not received a spirit of slavery leading to fear again, but I have received a spirit of adoption as a son, by which I cry out, "Abba! Father!"

Jesus, You delivered me, who, through fear of death, had been living all my life as a slave to constant dread. I receive the gift You left to me — peace of mind and heart! And the peace You give isn't fragile like the peace the world gives. I cast away troubled thoughts, and I choose not to be afraid. I believe in God; I believe also in You.

Lord, You are my Light and my Salvation; You protect me from danger — whom shall I fear? When evil men come to destroy me, they will stumble and fall! Yes, though a mighty army marches against me, my heart shall know no fear! I am confident that You will save me.

Thank You, Holy Spirit, for bringing these things to my remembrance when I am tempted to be afraid. I will trust in my God. In the name of Jesus, I pray.

Scripture References

Psalm 56:3-5 TLB	Hebrews 2:15 TLB
2 Timothy 1:7,8 NAS	John 14:1,17 TLB
Romans 8:15 NAS	Psalm 27:1-3 TLB

Overcoming Discouragement

Introduction

**Moses returned to the Lord and said, "O
Lord, why have you brought trouble upon this
people? Is this why you sent me? Ever since I went
to Pharaoh to speak in your name, he has brought
trouble upon this people, and you have not
rescued your people at all."**

Exodus 5:22,23 NIV

Here in this passage, we find Moses discouraged,
complaining to God.

It is important that we approach God with integrity
in an attitude of humility. Because we fear making a
negative confession, we sometimes cross the line of
honesty into the line of denial and delusion.

Let's be honest. God already knows what we are
feeling. He can handle our anger, complaints, and disap-
pointments. He understands us. He is aware of our
human frailties (Ps. 103:14) and can be touched with
the feelings of our infirmities (Heb. 4:15).

Whether your "trouble" is a business failure,
abandonment, depression, mental disorder, chemical
imbalance, oppression, a marriage problem, a child who

is in a strange land of drugs and alcohol, financial disaster, or anything else, the following prayer is for you.

Sometimes when you are in the midst of discouragement it is difficult to remember that you have ever known any Scripture. I admonish you to read this prayer aloud until you recognize the reality of God's Word in your spirit, soul, and body. Remember, God is watching over His Word to perform it (Jer. 1:12 AMP). He will perfect that which concerns you (Ps. 138:8).

Prayer

Lord, I have exhausted all my possibilities for changing my situation and circumstances and have found that I am powerless to change. I believe; help me overcome my unbelief. All things are not possible with man, but all things are possible with You. I humble myself before You, and You will lift me up.

I have a great High Priest Who has gone through the heavens, Jesus Your Son, and I hold firmly to the faith I profess. My High Priest is able to sympathize with my weaknesses. He was tempted in every way, just as I am — yet was without sin. I approach Your throne of grace with confidence, so that I may receive mercy and find grace to help me in my time of need.

In the face of discouragement, disappointment, and anger, I choose to believe that Your Word to Moses is Your Word to me. You are mighty to deliver. Because of Your mighty hand, You will drive out the forces that have set themselves up against me. You are the Lord, Yahweh, the Promise-Keeper, the Almighty One. You appeared to Abraham, to Isaac, and to Jacob and established Your covenant with them.

Father, I believe that You have heard my groaning, my cries. I will live to see Your promises of deliverance fulfilled in my life. You have not forgotten one word of Your promise; You are a Covenant-Keeper.

It is You Who will bring me out from under the yoke of bondage and free me from being a slave to _____. You have redeemed me with an outstretched arm and with mighty acts of judgment. You have taken me as Your own, and You are my God. You are a Father to me. You have delivered me from the past that has held me in bondage and translated me into the Kingdom of love, peace, joy, and righteousness. I will no longer settle for the pain of the past. Where sin abounds, grace does much more abound.

Father, what You have promised, I will go and possess, in the name of Jesus. I am willing to take the chance, to take the risk, to get back into the good fight of faith. It is with patient endurance and steady and active persistence that I run the race, the appointed course that is set before me. I rebuke the spirit of fear for I am established in righteousness. Oppression and destruction shall not come near me. Behold, they may gather together and stir up strife, but it is not from You, Father. Whoever stirs up strife against me shall fall and surrender to me. I am more than a conqueror through Him Who loves me.

In His name I pray, amen.

Scripture References

*(This prayer is based on Exodus 5:22–6:11
and includes other verses where applicable.)*

Mark 9:24 NIV

Luke 18:27

1 Peter 5:6 NIV

Hebrews 4:14-16 NIV

Exodus 6:3,4 AMP

Genesis 49:22-26 AMP

1 Kings 8:56

Deuteronomy 26:8

Colossians 1:13

Romans 5:20

1 Timothy 6:12

Hebrews 12:1 AMP

Isaiah 54:14-16

Romans 8:37

Overcoming Intimidation

Father, I come to You in the name of Jesus, confessing that intimidation has caused me to stumble. I ask Your forgiveness for thinking of myself as inferior, for I am created in Your image, and I am Your workmanship. Jesus said that the Kingdom of God is in me. Therefore, the power that raised Jesus from the dead dwells in me and causes me to face life with hope and divine energy.

The Lord is my Light and my Salvation; whom shall I fear? The Lord is the strength of my life; of whom shall I be afraid? Lord, You said that You would never leave me or forsake me. Therefore, I can say without any doubt or fear that You are my Helper, and I am not afraid of anything that mere man can do to me. Greater is He Who is in me than he who is in the world. If God is for me, who can be against me? I am free from the fear of man and public opinion.

Father, You have not given me a spirit of timidity — of cowardice, of craven and cringing and fawning fear — but You have given me a spirit of power and of love and of a calm and well-balanced mind and discipline and self-control. I can do all things through Christ Who gives me the strength. Amen.

Scripture References

1 John 1:9	Ephesians 2:10
Luke 17:21	Ephesians 1:19,20
Colossians 1:29	Psalm 1:27
Hebrews 13:5	1 John 4:4
Romans 3:31	Proverbs 29:25
2 Timothy 1:7	Philippians 4:13

Overcoming a Sense of Hopelessness

Father, as Your child I boldly come before Your throne of grace that I may receive mercy and find grace to help in this time of need.

Father, I know that Your ears are open to my prayers. I ask that You listen to my prayer, O God, and hide not Yourself from my supplication!

I am calling upon You, my God, to rescue me. You redeem my life in peace from the battle of hopelessness that is against me. I cast my burden on You, Lord, [releasing the weight of it] and You sustain me; You will never allow the [consistently] righteous to be moved (made to slip, fall, or fail).

What time I am afraid, I will have confidence in and put my trust and reliance in You. By [Your help], God, I will praise Your Word; on You I lean, rely, and confidently put my trust; I will not fear.

You know my every sleepless night. Each tear and heartache is answered with Your promise. I am thanking You with all my heart. You pulled me from the brink of death, my feet from the cliff-edge of doom.

[What would have become of me], Lord, had I not believed that I would see Your goodness in the

land of the living! I wait and hope for and expect You;
I am brave and of good courage, and I let my heart be
stout and enduring. Yes, I wait for and hope for and
expect You.

Father, I give You all my worries and cares, for You
are always thinking about me and watching everything
that concerns me. I am well balanced and careful —
vigilant, watching out for attacks from Satan, my great
enemy. By Your grace I am standing firm, trusting You,
and I remember that other Christians all around the
world are going through these sufferings too. You, God,
are full of kindness through Christ and will give me
Your eternal glory.

In the name of Jesus I am an overcomer by the blood
of the Lamb and by the word of my testimony. Amen.

Scripture References

Hebrews 4:16

Psalm 55:1 MESSAGE

Psalm 55:1 AMP

Psalm 55:5 AMP

Psalm 55:16,18,22 AMP

Psalm 56:2,4 AMP

Psalm 56:5,8 MESSAGE

Psalm 56:13 MESSAGE

Psalm 27:13,14 AMP

1 Peter 5:7-9 AMP, TLB

Revelation 12:11

Letting Go of Bitterness

Introduction

In interviews with divorced men and women, I have been encouraged to write a prayer on overcoming bitterness.

Often, the injustice of the situation in which these people find themselves creates deep hurts, wounds in the spirit, and anger that is so near the surface the individuals involved risk sinking into the trap of bitterness and revenge. Their thoughts may turn inward as they consider the unfairness of the situation and dwell on how badly they have been treated.

In a family divorce situation, bitterness sometimes distorts ideas of what is best for the child/children involved. One parent (and sometimes both parents) will use the child/children against the other.

Unresolved anger often moves one marriage partner to hurt the one he or she holds responsible for the hurt and sense of betrayal which they feel.

There is healing available. There is a way of escape for all who will turn to the Healer, obeying Him and trusting Him.

Prayer

Father, life seems so unjust, so unfair. The pain of rejection is almost more than I can bear. My past relationships have ended in strife, anger, rejection, and separation.

Lord, help me to let go of all bitterness and indignation and wrath (passion, rage, bad temper) and resentment (anger, animosity).

You are the One Who binds up and heals the brokenhearted. I receive Your anointing that destroys every yoke of bondage. I receive emotional healing by faith, and I thank You for giving me the grace to stand firm until the process is complete.

Thank You for wise counselors. I acknowledge the Holy Spirit as my wonderful Counselor. Thank You for helping me work out my salvation with fear and trembling, for it is You, Father, Who work in me to will and to act according to Your good purpose.

In the name of Jesus, I choose to forgive those who have wronged me. I purpose to live a life of forgiveness because You have forgiven me. With the help of the Holy Spirit, I get rid of all bitterness, rage, and anger, brawling and slander, along with every form of malice. I desire to be kind and compassionate to others, forgiving them, just as in Christ You forgave me.

With the help of the Holy Spirit, I make every effort to live in peace with all men and to be holy, for I know that without holiness no one will see You, Lord. I purpose to see to it that I do not miss Your grace and that no bitter root grows up within me to cause trouble.

I will watch and pray that I enter not into temptation or cause others to stumble.

Thank You, Father, that You watch over Your Word to perform it and that whom the Son has set free is free indeed. I declare that I have overcome resentment and bitterness by the blood of the Lamb and by the word of my testimony.

In Jesus' name, amen.

Scripture References

Ephesians 4:31 AMP

Luke 4:18

Isaiah 10:27

Proverbs 11:14

John 15:26 AMP

Philippians 2:12,13 NIV

Matthew 5:44

Ephesians 4:31,32 NIV

Hebrews 12:14,15 NIV

Matthew 26:41

Romans 14:21

Jeremiah 1:12 AMP

John 8:36

Revelation 12:11

Health and Healing

Father, in the name of Jesus, I come before You asking You to heal me. It is written that the prayer of faith will save the sick, and the Lord will raise him up. And if I have committed sins, I will be forgiven. I let go of all unforgiveness, resentment, anger, and bad feelings toward anyone.

My body is the temple of the Holy Spirit, and I desire to be in good health. I seek truth that will make me free — both spiritual and natural *(good eating habits, medications if necessary, and appropriate rest and exercise).* You bought me at a price, and I desire to glorify You in my spirit and my body — they both belong to You.

Thank You, Father, for sending Your Word to heal me and deliver me from all my destructions. Jesus, You are the Word Who became flesh and dwelt among us. You bore my griefs (pains) and carried my sorrows (sickness). You were pierced through for my transgressions, crushed for my iniquities, the chastening for my wellbeing fell upon You, and by Your scourging I am healed.

Father, I give attention to Your words and incline my ear to Your sayings. I will not let them depart from my sight, but I will keep them in the midst of my heart, for they are life and health to my whole body.

Since the Spirit of Him Who raised Jesus from the dead dwells in me, He Who raised Christ from the dead will also give life to my mortal body through His Spirit Who dwells in me.

Thank You that I will prosper and be in health, even as my soul prospers. Amen.

Scripture References

James 5:15 NKJV   Proverbs 4:21,22 NAS

1 Corinthians 6:19,20   Psalm 103:3-5 NAS

Psalm 107:20   Romans 8:11 NKJV

John 1:14   3 John 2

Isaiah 53:4,5 NAS

Safety

Father, in the name of Jesus, I thank You that You watch over Your Word to perform it. I thank You that I dwell in the secret place of the Most High and that I remain stable and fixed under the shadow of the Almighty whose power no foe can withstand.

Father, You are my Refuge and my Fortress. *No evil shall befall me — no accident shall overtake me — nor any plague or calamity come near my home.* You give Your angels special charge over me, to accompany and defend and preserve me in all my ways of obedience and service. They are encamped around about me.

Father, You are my confidence, firm and strong. You keep my foot from being caught in a trap or hidden danger. Father, You give me safety and ease me — *Jesus is my safety!*

Traveling — As I go, I say, "Let me pass over to the other side," and I have what I say. I walk on my way securely and in confident trust, for my heart and mind are firmly fixed and stayed on You, and I am kept in perfect peace.

Sleeping — Father, I sing for joy upon my bed because You sustain me. In peace I lie down and sleep, for You alone, Lord, make me dwell in safety. I lie down and I am not afraid. My sleep is sweet for You give blessings to me in sleep. Thank You, Father, in Jesus' name. Amen.

Continue to feast and meditate upon all of Psalm 91 for yourself and your loved ones!

Scripture References

Jeremiah 1:12	Proverbs 3:23 AMP
Psalm 91:1,2 AMP	Psalm 112:7
Psalm 91:10 AMP	Isaiah 26:3
Psalm 91:11 AMP	Psalm 149:5
Psalm 34:7	Psalm 3:5
Proverbs 3:26 AMP	Psalm 4:8 AMP
Isaiah 49:25	Proverbs 3:24
Mark 4:35	Psalm 127:2

Peaceful Sleep

Father, thank You for peaceful sleep, and for Your
angels that encamp around us who fear You. You deliver
us and keep us safe. The angels excel in strength, do
Your Word and heed the voice of Your Word. You give
Your angels charge over me, to keep me in all my ways.

I bring every thought, every imagination, and every
dream into the captivity and obedience of Jesus Christ.
Father, I thank You that even as I sleep my heart counsels me and reveals to me Your purpose and plan. Thank
You for sweet sleep, for You promised Your beloved
sweet sleep. Therefore, my heart is glad, and my spirit
rejoices. My body and soul rest and confidently dwell in
safety. Amen.

Scripture References

Psalm 103:20   Psalm 92:11

Prosperity

Father, I come to You in the name of Jesus, concerning my financial situation. You are a very present help in trouble, and You are more than enough. Your Word declares that You shall supply all my need according to Your riches in glory by Christ Jesus.

(If you have not been giving tithes and offerings, include the statement of repentance in your prayer.) Forgive me for robbing You in tithes and offerings. I repent and purpose to bring all my tithes into the storehouse that there may be food in Your house. Thank You for wise financial counselors and teachers who are teaching me the principles of good stewardship.

Lord of hosts, You said, "Try Me now in this, and I will open the windows of heaven and pour out such a blessing for you that there will not be room enough to receive it." You will rebuke the devourer for my sake, and my heart is filled with thanksgiving.

Lord, my God, I shall remember that it is You Who gives me the power to get wealth that You may establish Your covenant. In the name of Jesus, I worship You only, and I will have no others gods before me.

You are able to make all grace — every favor and earthly blessing — come to me in abundance, so that I am always, and in all circumstances, furnished in abundance for every good work and charitable donation. Amen.

Scripture References

Psalm 56:1

Philippians 4:19

Malachi 3: 8-12

Deuteronomy 8:18,19

2 Corinthians 9:8 AMP

To Receive the Infilling of the Holy Spirit

My Heavenly Father, I am Your child, for I believe in my heart that Jesus has been raised from the dead and I have confessed Him as my Lord.

Jesus said, "How much more shall your Heavenly Father give the Holy Spirit to those who ask Him?" I ask You now in the name of Jesus to fill me with the Holy Spirit. I step into the fullness and power that I desire in the name of Jesus. I confess that I am a Spirit-filled Christian. As I yield my vocal organs, I expect to speak in tongues for the Spirit gives me utterance in the name of Jesus. Praise the Lord! Amen.

Scripture References

John 14:16,17	Acts 10:44-46
Luke 11:13	Acts 19:2,5,6
Acts 1:8a	1 Corinthians14:2-15
Acts 2:4	1 Corinthians 14:18,27
Acts 2:32,33,39	Ephesians 6:18
Acts 8:12-17	Jude 1:20

When Desiring To Have a Baby

Our Father, my spouse and I bow our knees unto
You. Father of our Lord Jesus Christ of whom the
whole family in heaven and on earth is named, we pray
that You would grant to us according to the riches of
Your glory, to be strengthened with might by Your
Spirit in the inner man. Christ dwells in our hearts by
faith, that we — being rooted and grounded in love —
may be able to comprehend with all the saints what is
the breadth, and length, and depth, and height of the
love of Christ, which passes knowledge, that we might
be filled with all the fullness of God.

Hallelujah, we praise You, O Lord, for You give
children to the childless wife, so that she becomes a
happy mother. And we thank You that You are the One
Who is building our family. As Your children and
inheritors through Jesus Christ, we receive Your gift —
the fruit of the womb, Your child as our reward.

We praise You, our Father, in Jesus' name, for we
know that whatsoever we ask, we receive of You,

because we keep Your commandments, and do those things which are pleasing in Your sight.

Thank You, Father, that we are a fruitful vine within our house; our children will be like olive shoots around our table. Thus shall we be blessed because we fear the Lord.

In Jesus' name we pray, amen.

Scripture References

Ephesians 3:14-19   1 John 3:22,23 AMP

Psalm 113:9 AMP   Psalm 128:3,4 AMP

Psalm 127:3

Godly Order in Pregnancy and Childbirth

Father, in Jesus' name, I confess Your Word this day over my pregnancy and the birth of my child. I ask that You will quickly perform Your Word trusting that it will not go out from You and return to You void, but rather that it will accomplish that which pleases You. Your Word is quick and powerful, and discerns my heart intentions and the thoughts of my mind.

Right now I put on the whole armor of God so that I may be able to stand against the tricks and traps of the devil. I recognize that my fight is not with flesh and blood, but against principalities, powers, and the rulers of darkness and spiritual wickedness in high places. God, I stand above all, taking the shield of faith and being able to quench the attacks of the devil with Your mighty power. I stand in faith during this pregnancy and birth, not giving any room to fear, but possessing power, love, and a sound mind as Your Word promises in 2 Timothy 1:7.

Heavenly Father, I confess that You are my refuge; I trust You during this pregnancy and childbirth. I am

thankful that You have put angels at watch over me
and my unborn child. I cast all the care and burden of
this pregnancy over on You, Lord. Your grace is sufficient for me through this pregnancy; You strengthen
my weaknesses.

Father, Your Word declares that my unborn child
was created in Your image, fearfully and wonderfully
made to praise You. You have made me a joyful mother,
and I am blessed with a heritage from You as my
reward. I commit this child to You, Father, and pray that
he will grow and call me blessed.

I am not afraid of pregnancy or childbirth because I
am fixed and trusting upon You, Father. I believe that
my pregnancy and childbirth will be void of all problems. Thank You, Father, that all decisions regarding my
pregnancy and delivery will be godly, that the Holy
Spirit will intervene. Lord, You are my dwelling place
and I rest in the knowledge that evil will not come near
me and no sickness or infirmity will strike me or my
unborn child. I know that Jesus died on the cross to take
away my sickness and pain. Having accepted Your Son
Jesus as my Savior, I confess that my child will be born
healthy and completely whole. Thank You, Father, for

the law of the Spirit of life in Christ Jesus that has made me and my child free from the law of sin and death!

Father, thank You for protecting me and my baby and for our good health. Thank You for hearing and answering my prayers. Amen.

Scripture References

Jeremiah 1:12	Proberbs 31:28
Isaiah 55:11	Psalm 112:7
Hebrews 4:12	Psalm 91:1,10
Ephesians 6:11,12,16	Matthew 8:17
Psalm 91:2,11	Romans 8:2
1 Peter 5:7	James 4:7
2 Corinthians 12:9	Ephesians 6:12
Genesis 1:26	John 4:13
Psalm 139:14	Matthew 18:18
Psalm 113:9	Jeremiah 33:3
Psalm 127:3	

Adopting a Child

Father, in Jesus' name, we come boldly before Your throne of grace that we may receive mercy and find grace to help in our time of need. We are trusting in You, and seek to do good; so that we may dwell in the land, and feed surely on Your faithfulness.

We delight ourselves also in You, and You give us the desires and secret petitions of our heart. We believe our desire to adopt a child is from You, and we are willing to assume the responsibility of rearing this child in the ways of the Master.

Father, we commit our way to You [roll and repose each care of our load on You]. Our confidence is in You, and You will bring this adoption to pass according to Your purpose and plan.

Lord, Your Son Jesus demonstrated Your love for children when He said, **"Let the children alone, don't prevent them from coming to me. God's kingdom is made up of people like these"** (Matt. 19:14 MESSAGE). Then, He laid hands on them and blessed them.

Use us as Your instruments of peace and righteousness to bless this child. We purpose in our hearts to
train this child up in the way that he/she should go.

Lord, we are embracing this child (Your best
gift) as our very own with Your love, as Jesus said,
**"Whoever embraces one of these children as I do
embraces me, and far more than me — God who
sent me"** (Mark 9:37 MESSAGE).

Father, take this child up and be a Father and
Mother to him/her as we extend our hands and our
hearts to embrace him/her. Thank You for the blood of
Jesus that gives protection to this one whom we love.

We thank You for the man and woman who
conceived this child, and pray that You will bless them,
cause Your face to shine upon them, and be merciful to
them. If they do not know Jesus, we ask You, the Lord
of the harvest, to send forth laborers to share truth with
them that they may come out of the snare of the devil.

Mercy and truth are written upon the tablets of our
hearts, and You cause us to find favor and good understanding with You and with man — the adoption
agency staff, the judges, and all those who are involved

in this decision-making process. May everyone be careful that they do not despise one of these little ones over whom they have jurisdiction — for they have angels who see Your face continually in heaven.

We believe that all our words are righteous (upright and in right standing with You, Father). By our long forbearing and calmness of spirit those in authority are persuaded, and our soft speech breaks down the most bonelike resistance.

Lord, we are looking to You as our Great Counselor and Mighty Advocate. We ask for Your wisdom for us and our attorneys.

Father, contend with those who contend with us, and give safety to our child and ease him/her day by day. We are calling on You, in the name of Jesus, and You will answer us and show us great and mighty things. No weapon formed against us and this adoption shall prosper, and any tongue that rises against us in judgment we shall show to be in the wrong. This [peace, righteousness, security, and triumph over opposition] is our inheritance as Your children.

Father, we believe; therefore we have spoken. May it be done unto us according to Your Word.

In Jesus' name, amen.

Scripture References

Hebrews 4:16	Matthew 18:10 PHILLIPS
Psalm 37:3	Proverbs 8:8 AMP
Psalm 37:4 AMP	Proverbs 25:15 AMP
Ephesians 6:4 MESSAGE	James 1:5
Psalm 37:5 AMP	Isaiah 49:25
Proverbs 22:6	Jeremiah 33:3
Psalm 67:1	Isaiah 54:17 AMP
Matthew 9:38	Psalm 116:10
2 Timothy 2:26	Luke 1:38
Proverbs 3:3,4	

Part II

Prayers for Relationships

Developing Healthy Friendships

Father, help me to meet new friends — friends who will encourage me. May I find in these friendships the companionship and fellowship You have ordained for me. I know that You are my source of love, companionship, and friendship. Your love and friendship are expressed through my relationship with You and members of the Body of Christ.

According to Proverbs 27:17 CEV, iron sharpens iron, so friends sharpen the minds of each other. As we learn from each other, may we find a worthy purpose in our relationship. Keep me well-balanced in my friendships, so that I will always please You rather than pleasing other people.

I ask for divine connections — good friendships ordained by You. Thank You for the courage and grace to let go of detrimental friendships. I ask and receive, by faith, discernment for developing healthy relationships. Your Word says that two are better than one, because if one falls, there will be someone to lift that person up.

Father, You know the hearts of people, so I won't be deceived by outward appearances. Bad friendships corrupt good morals. Thank You for quality friends who help me build a stronger character and draw me closer to You. Help me be a friend to others and to love my friends at all times. I will laugh with those who laugh, I will rejoice with those who rejoice, and I will weep with those who weep. Teach me what I need to know to be a quality friend.

Develop in me a fun personality and a good sense of humor. Help me to relax around people and to be myself — the person You created me to be. Instruct my heart and mold my character, that I may be faithful and trustworthy over the friendships You are sending into my life.

Father, Your Son Jesus is my best Friend. He is a Friend Who sticks closer than a brother. He defined the standard when He said in John 15:13, **Greater love hath no man than this, that a man lay down his life for his friends.**

Thank You, Lord, that I can entrust myself and my need for friends into Your keeping. I submit to the leadership of the Holy Spirit, in the name of Jesus. Amen.

Scripture References

Proverbs 13:20 NIV	1 Corinthians 15:33 AMP
Ephesians 5:30 NIV	James 1:17 NIV
Philippians 2:2,3 NIV	Proverbs 17:17
Proverbs 13:20 NIV	Romans 12:15
Psalm 84:11 NIV	Proverbs 18:24
Ecclesiastes 4:9,10 NIV	Psalm 37:4,5 NIV

This prayer is composed of Scriptures and writings taken from "Meeting New Friends," *Prayers That Avail Much for Teens!* (Tulsa: Harrison House, 1991), pp. 50-52.

Maintaining Good Relations

Father, in the name of Jesus, I will not withhold good from those to whom it is due [its rightful owners], when it is in the power of my hand to do it. I will render to all men their dues. I will [pay] taxes to whom taxes are due, revenue to whom revenue is due, respect to whom respect is due, and honor to whom honor is due.

I will not lose heart and grow weary and faint in acting nobly and doing nobly and right, for in due season I shall reap, if I do not loosen and relax my courage and faint. So then, as occasion and opportunity open up to me, I will do good [morally] to all people [not only being useful or profitable to them, but also doing what is for their spiritual good and advantage]. I am mindful to be a blessing, especially to those of the household of faith [those who belong to God's family with me, the believers].

I will not contend with a man for no reason — when he has done me no wrong. If possible, as far as it depends on me, I purpose to live at peace with everyone. Amen.

Scripture References

Proverbs 3:27 AMP   Proverbs 3:30 AMP

Romans 13:7 AMP   Romans 12:18 AMP

Galatians 6:9,10 AMP

Improving Communication Skills

Introduction

Lack of communication skills is one of the greatest hindrances to healthy relationships. Most of the time, when we pray, we are seeking change. We cannot change others, but we can submit to the constant ministry of transformation by the Holy Spirit (Rom. 12:1,2).

Prayer prepares us for change. Change produces change, which may be uncomfortable. If we will move through the discomfort, God will work with us, leading us out of our self-developed defense mechanisms into a place of victory. In this place He heals our brokenness, becomes our defense and our vindication. We are enabled to submit to the Champion of our salvation, which we are working out with fear and trembling (Phil. 2:12).

Adults who grew up in judgmental, critical homes where they were never allowed to express themselves sometimes carry much hurt and anger into their relationships. Often, they were not permitted to have their own feelings without being condemned; they were not permitted to explore any ideas different from their parents or caregivers. There was an eye watching their every move. Any punishment they received was justified. Their parents were incapable of making a mistake.

Adult children of religiously rigid environments were led to believe that any slip, error in judgment, or mistake was a sin that would send them straight to hell; the parent's religious doctrine was the only way to heaven; and to deviate from it would lead to destruction. Forgiveness could be attained only after much sorrow, penance, and retribution. Death before the completion of repentance led to an eternity in hell.

People raised in such oppressive home environments were never allowed to find themselves or to travel their own individual spiritual journeys leading to truth. Their parents, especially the father-figure in the home, was God in the flesh. Conflict resolution was never taught or practiced. Whatever the head of the household said was law — and disobedience to his law was not discussed, but beaten out of the child. The wife was subservient and was not allowed to question the dictates of the husband.

When these adults marry, they often feel that they have finally found a platform from which to express themselves. They have escaped a place of abiding fear, constant condemnation, and continual criticism. Having no communication skills, they often have difficulty expressing themselves properly. When anyone disagrees with them, they tend to react as they were taught. Only now, the marriage partner or friend does not submit to dogmatic, manipulative words. Frustration develops. The adult child seeks to make himself or herself understood, resulting in more frustration. Anger is fed, and the individual continues to be in bondage to the idea that he or she should never have been born. The person either retreats to a silent corner, refusing to talk, or uses words to build walls of defense — shutting others out. He or she resides inside emotional isolation, attempting to remove himself or herself from more hurt and criticism.

There is a way of escape. God sent His Word to heal us and to deliver us from all our destructions (Ps. 107:20). We must determine to listen, to learn, and to change with the help of the Holy Spirit — our Teacher, our Guide, and our Intercessor. The anointing

is upon Jesus to bind up and heal our emotional wounds
(Luke 4:18). His anointing destroys every yoke of
bondage (Isa. 10:27), setting the captives free.

Prayer

Father, I am Your child. Jesus said that if I pray to
You in secret, You will reward me openly.

Father, I desire with all my heart to walk in love,
but I am ever sabotaging my own efforts and failing in
my relationships. I know that without faith it is
impossible to please and be satisfactory to You. I am
coming near to You, believing that You exist and that
You are the rewarder of those who earnestly and diligently seek You.

Show "me" to me. Uncover — bring everything to
the light — when anything is exposed and reproved by
the light, it is made visible and clear; and where everything is visible and clear, there is light.

Heal the past wounds and hurts which have
controlled my behavior and my speech. Teach me to
guard my heart with all diligence, for out of it flow the
very issues of life. Teach me to speak the truth in love in

my home, in my church, with my friends and in all my relationships. Also, help me to realize that others have a right to express themselves. Help me to make room for their ideas, their opinions, even when they are different from mine.

Words are powerful. The power of life and death is in the tongue, and You said that I would eat the fruit of it.

Father, I realize that words can be creative or destructive. A word out of my mouth may seem of no account, but it can accomplish nearly anything — or destroy it! A careless or wrongly placed word out of my mouth can set off a forest fire. By my speech I can ruin the world, turn harmony to chaos, throw mud on a reputation, send the whole world up in smoke, and go up in smoke with it, smoke right from the pit of hell. This is scary!

Father, forgive me for speaking curses. I reacted out of past hurts and unresolved anger. At times I am dogmatic, even boasting that I am wise; sometimes, unknowingly I have twisted the truth to make myself sound wise; at times I have tried to look better than others, or get the better of another; my words have contributed to things falling apart. My human anger is misdirected and works unrighteousness.

Father, forgive me. I cannot change myself, but I am willing to change and walk in the wisdom that is from above.

Father, I submit to that wisdom from above that begins with a holy life and is characterized by getting along with others. It is gentle and reasonable, overflowing with mercy and blessings, not hot one day and cold the next, not two-faced. Use me as Your instrument to develop a healthy, robust community that lives right with You. I will enjoy its results only if I do the hard work of getting along with others, treating them with dignity and honor.

With the help of the Holy Spirit and by Your grace, I will not let any unwholesome talk come out of my mouth, but only what is helpful for building others up according to their needs, that it may benefit those who listen.

My heart overflows with a goodly theme; I address my psalm to You, the King. My tongue is like the pen of a ready writer. Mercy and kindness shut out all hatred and selfishness, and truth shuts out all deliberate hypocrisy or falsehood; and I bind them about my neck, write them upon the tablet of my heart.

I speak excellent and princely things; and the opening of my lips shall be for right things. My mouth shall utter truth, and wrongdoing is detestable and loathsome to my lips. All the words of my mouth are righteous (upright and in right standing with You, Lord); there is nothing contrary to truth or crooked in them. My tongue is as choice silver, and my lips feed and guide many. I open my mouth in skillful and godly wisdom, and on my tongue is the law of kindness [giving counsel and instruction].

Father, thank You for loving me unconditionally. I thank You for sending Your Son Jesus to be my Friend and elder Brother and for giving me Your Holy Spirit to teach me and to bring all things to my remembrance. I am an overcomer by the blood of the Lamb and by the word of my testimony.

In the name of Jesus I pray, amen.

Scripture References

1 John 3:1	Ephesians 4:29 NIV
Matthew 6:6	Psalm 45:1 AMP
Hebrews 11:6 AMP	Proverbs 3:3 AMP
Ephesians 5:13 AMP	Proverbs 8:6-8 AMP
Proverbs 4:23	Proverbs 10:20,21 AMP
Ephesians 4:15	Proverbs 31:26 AMP
Proverbs 18:21	Romans 8:31-39 NIV
James 3:5,6 MESSAGE	Hebrews 2:11 NIV
James 3:9-16 MESSAGE	John 15:15 NIV
James 3:17	John 14:26
James 3:17,18 MESSAGE	Revelation 12:11

Finding Favor With Others

Father, in the name of Jesus, You make Your face to shine upon and enlighten _____ and are gracious (kind, merciful, and giving favor) to him/her. _____ is the head and not the tail. _____ is above only and not beneath.

Thank You for favor for _____ who seeks Your Kingdom and Your righteousness and diligently seeks good. _____ is a blessing to You, Lord, and is a blessing to _____ *(name them: family, neighbors, business associates, etc.)*. Grace (favor) is with _____ who loves the Lord Jesus in sincerity. _____ extends favor, honor, and love to _____*(names)*. _____ is flowing in Your Love, Father. You are pouring out upon _____ the spirit of favor. You crown him/her with glory and honor for he/she is Your child — Your workmanship.

_____ is a success today. _____ is someone very special with You, Lord. _____ is growing in the Lord — waxing strong in spirit. Father, You give _____ knowledge and skill in all learning and wisdom.

You bring _____ to find favor, compassion, and loving-kindness with _____ *(names).*
_____ obtains favor in the sight of all who look upon him/her this day in the name of Jesus.
_____ is filled with Your fullness — rooted and grounded in love. You are doing exceeding abundantly above all that _____ asks or thinks for Your mighty power is taking over in _____.

Thank You, Father, that _____ is well-favored by You and by man in Jesus' name! Amen.

Scripture References

Numbers 6:25	Psalm 8:5
Deuteronomy 28:13	Ephesians 2:10
Matthew 6:33	Luke 2:40
Proverbs 11:27	Daniel 1:17
Ephesians 6:24	Daniel 1:9
Luke 6:38	Esther 2:15,17
Zachariah 12:10	Ephesians 3:19,20

Finding a Mate

Introduction

In our ministry we hear from many men and women who desire to be married. If that is your desire, we encourage you to ask the Lord to prepare you for marriage. Submit to God's future plans for your life, and purpose to please Him. Do not make your deliberations, without knowing His will, at the expense of your personal spiritual growth and transformation. Going from glory to glory (2 Cor. 3:18) is not dependent on having a spouse.

Most of the time, each partner brings a lot of emotional baggage into the marriage relationship. As you prepare for marriage, remember that the anointing that was upon Jesus (Luke 4:18,19) is within you. This anointing will destroy every yoke of bondage (Isa. 10:27) as God exposes emotional wounds and heals your brokenness.

Knowing the reality of your completeness in Christ Jesus will enable you to enter into a healthy relationship, one in which both you and your partner will grow

together spiritually and in every other area of life.
Seeking first the Kingdom of God and His righteousness (Matt. 6:33), doing those things that are pleasing
in His sight (1 John 3:22), will prepare you to be the
person designed by Him to fulfill the role of husband
or wife.

This prayer is written for your own growth and
benefit.

Prayer

Father, I come before You in the name of Jesus,
asking for Your will to be done in my life as I look to
You for a marriage partner. I submit to the constant
ministry of transformation by the Holy Spirit, making
my petition known to You.

Prepare me for marriage by bringing everything to
light that has been hidden — wounded emotions, walls
of denial, emotional isolation, silence or excessive
talking, anger or rigidity *[name any wall that separates you
from healthy relationships and God's love and grace]*. The
weapons of my warfare are not carnal, but mighty
through You, Lord, to the pulling down of strongholds.

I know the One in Whom I have placed my confidence, and I am perfectly certain that the work, whether I remain unmarried or marry, is safe in Your hands until that day.

Because I love You, Lord, and because I am called according to Your plan, everything that happens to me fits into a pattern for good. In Your foreknowledge, You chose me to bear the family likeness of Your Son. You chose me long ago; when the time came You called me, You made me righteous in Your sight, and then lifted me to the splendor of life as Your child.

I lay aside every weight, and the sins which so easily ensnare me, and run with endurance the race that is set before me, looking unto Jesus, the Author and Finisher of my faith, Who for the joy that was set before Him endured the cross, despising the shame, and has sat down at the right hand of the throne of God. I consider Him Who endured such hostility from sinners against Himself, lest I become weary and discouraged in my soul. He makes intercession for me.

I turn my back on the turbulent desires of youth and give my positive attention to goodness, integrity,

love, and peace in company with all those who approach
You, Lord, in sincerity. I have nothing to do with silly
and ill-informed controversies which lead inevitably to
strife. As Your servant, I am not a person of strife. I seek
to be kind to all, ready and able to teach. I seek to be
tolerant and have the ability gently to correct those who
oppose Your message.

Father, I desire and earnestly seek (aim at and strive
after) first of all Your Kingdom and Your righteousness
(Your way of doing and being right), and then all these
things taken together will be given me besides. So I do
not worry and will not be anxious about tomorrow.

I am persuaded that I can trust You because You
first loved me. You chose me in Christ before the foundation of the world. In Him the whole fullness of
Deity (the Godhead) continues to dwell in bodily form
[giving complete expression of the divine nature] and I
am in Him, made full and have come to the fullness of
life [in Christ].

I am filled with the Godhead — Father, Son, and
Holy Spirit — and I reach toward full spiritual stature.
And He (Christ) is the Head of all rule and authority

[of every angelic principality and power]. So, because of Jesus, I am complete; Jesus is my Lord.

I come before You, Father, expressing my desire for a Christian mate. I petition that Your will be done in my life. Now I enter into that blessed rest by adhering to, trusting in, and relying on You.

In Jesus' name, amen.

Scripture References

Matthew 6:10	Matthew 6:33,34 AMP
1 Corinthians 4:5	1 John 4:19
2 Corinthians 10:4	Ephesians 1:4
2 Timothy 1:12 PHILLIPS	Colossians 2:9,10 AMP
Romans 8:28-30 PHILLIPS	Matthew 6:10
Hebrews 12:1-3 NKJ	Hebrews 4:10
2 Timothy 2:22-25	John 14:1 AMP
PHILLIPS	Romans 8:34

Preparing Self for Marriage

Father, sometimes being single can be so lonely, so painful. Seeing people in pairs, laughing and having fun, makes me feel even more alone and different.

Lord, please comfort me in these times. Help me to deal with my feelings and thoughts in an appropriate way. Help me to remember to work hard on myself, so that I will be whole and mature when You bring the right person into my life.

Help me to remember that this is a time of preparation for the day when I will be joined to another human being for life. Show me how to be responsible for myself and how to allow others to be responsible for themselves.

Teach me about boundaries, what they are and how to establish them instead of walls. Teach me about love, Your love, and how to speak the truth in love, as Jesus did.

Father, I don't want to be a hindrance to my future spouse, to You, or to myself. Help me to take a good

look at myself, at my self-image. Lead me to people —
teachers, preachers, counselors — and to things —
books, tapes, seminars — anyone and anything You
can use to teach me Your ways of being and doing
right and being whole.

Teach me how to choose the mate You would have
for me. Give me the wisdom I need to see clearly, and
not to be double-minded. Help me to recognize the
qualities You would have me look for in a mate.

Father, thank You for revealing to me that the
choice of a mate is not to be based only on emotions
and feelings, but that You have very definite guidelines
in the Bible for me to use. I know that when I put these
principles into practice, I will save myself a lot of pain
and trouble.

Thank You that You are not trying to make things
hard for me, but that You know me better than I know
myself. You know my situation — You know the beginning from the end. You know the qualities and attributes that are needed in another person that will make
me happy in our shared life together and that person
happy with me.

I pray that You will keep my foot from being caught in a hidden trap or danger. I cast the care of this decision on You, knowing that You will cause my thoughts to come in line with Your will so that my plans will be established and succeed.

In Jesus' name I pray, amen.

Scripture References

1 Corinthians 1:3,4 NIV James 1:5-8

Ephesians 4:15 Proverbs 3:26 AMP

Matthew 6:33 AMP Proverbs 16:3 AMP

Compatibility in Marriage

Father, in the name of Jesus, the love of God is shed abroad in our hearts by the Holy Spirit Who indwells us. Therefore, my spouse and I are learning to endure long and are patient and kind; we are never envious and never boil over with jealousy. We are not boastful or vainglorious, and we do not display ourselves haughtily. We are not conceited or arrogant and inflated with pride. We are not rude and unmannerly, and we do not act unbecomingly. We do not insist on our own rights or our own way, for we are not self-seeking or touchy or fretful or resentful. We take no account of the evil done to us and pay no attention to a suffered wrong. We do not rejoice at injustice and unrighteousness, but we rejoice when right and truth prevail.

We bear up under anything and everything that comes. We are ever ready to believe the best of each other. Our hopes are fadeless under all circumstances. We endure everything without weakening. *Our love never fails* — it never fades out or becomes obsolete or comes to an end.

We are no longer children tossed to and fro, carried about with every wind of doctrine, but we speak the truth in love, dealing truly and living truly. We are enfolded in love, growing up in every way and in all things. We esteem and delight in one another, forgiving one another readily and freely as God in Christ has forgiven us. We are imitators of God and copy His example as well-beloved children imitate their father.

Thank You, Father, that our marriage grows stronger each day because it is founded on Your Word and on Your kind of love. We give You the praise for it all, Father, in the name of Jesus. Amen.

Scripture References

1 Corinthians 13:4-8 AMP   Ephesians 4:15,32

1 Corinthians 14:1   Ephesians 5:1,2

Wives

In the name of Jesus, I cultivate inner beauty, the gentle, gracious kind that God delights in. I choose to be a good, loyal wife to my husband and address him with respect. I will not be over anxious and intimidated. I purpose to be, by God's grace, agreeable, sympathetic, loving, compassionate, and humble. I will be a blessing and also receive blessings.

By the grace of God, I yield to the constant ministry of transformation by the Holy Spirit. I am being transformed into a gracious woman who retains honor, and a virtuous woman who is a crown to my husband. I purpose to walk wisely that I may build my house. Houses and riches are the inheritance of fathers, and a prudent wife is from the Lord. In Christ I have redemption through His blood, the forgiveness of sins, according to the riches of His grace which He made to abound toward me in all wisdom and prudence.

Holy Spirit, I ask You to help me understand and support my husband in ways that show my support for Christ.* Teach me to function so that I preserve my own personality while responding to his desires. We are one flesh, and I realize that this unity of persons that preserves individuality is a mystery, but that is how it is when we are united to Christ. So I will keep on loving my husband and let the miracle keep happening!

Just as my husband gives me what is due me, I seek to be fair to my husband. I share my rights with my husband.

Strength and dignity are my clothing, and my position in my household is strong. My family is in readiness for the future. The bread of idleness (gossip, discontent, and self-pity) I will not eat. I choose to conduct the affairs of my household wisely, realizing that wisdom from above is pure, peaceable, gentle, willing to yield, full of mercy and good fruits, without partiality and without hypocrisy. Amen.

Scripture References

Matthew 16:19 NKJV

1 Peter 3:1-5,8,9 MESSAGE

Psalm 51:10 NKJV

2 Corinthians 3:18

Proverbs 11:16

Proverbs 12:4

Proverbs 14:1

Proverbs 19:14

Ephesians 1:7,8 NKJV

Ephesians 5:22-33* MESSAGE

1 Corinthians 7:2-5** PHILLIPS

Proverbs 31:25-27 AMP

James 3:17,18 NKJV

* *The Message* and Paraphrase *The Heart of Paul,* Ben Campbell Johnson, © 1976, A Great Love, Inc., Toccoa, GA 30577.
** *The New Testament in Modern English,* J.B. Phillips

The Unborn Child

Father, in Jesus' name, I thank You for my unborn child. I treasure this child as a gift from You. My child was created in Your image, perfectly healthy and complete. You have known my child since conception and know the path he/she will take with his/her life. I ask Your blessing upon him/her and stand and believe in his/her salvation through Jesus Christ.

When You created man and woman, You called them blessed and crowned them with glory and honor. It is in You, Father, that my child will live and move, and have his/her being. He/She is Your offspring and will come to worship and praise You.

Heavenly Father, I thank and praise You for the great things You have done and are continuing to do. I am in awe at the miracle of life You have placed inside of me. Thank You! Amen.

Scripture References

Psalm 127:3	Matthew 18:18
Genesis 1:26	John 14:13
Jeremiah 1:5	Galatians 3:13
2 Peter 3:9	1 John 3:8
Psalm 8:5	Psalm 91:1
Acts 17:28,29	

The Children

Father, in the name of Jesus, I pray and confess Your Word over my children and surround them with my faith — faith in Your Word that You watch over it to perform it! I confess and believe that my children are disciples of Christ taught of the Lord and obedient to Your will. Great is the peace and undisturbed composure of my children, because You, God, contend with that which contends with my children, and You give them safety and ease them.

Father, You will perfect that which concerns me. *I commit and cast the care of my children once and for all over on You, Father.* They are in Your hands, and I am positively persuaded that You are able to guard and keep that which I have committed to You. You are more than enough!

I confess that my children obey their parents in the Lord as His representatives, because this is just and right. My children _____ honor, esteem, and value as precious their parents; for this is the first commandment with a promise: that all may be well

with my children and that they may live long on earth. I
believe and confess that my children choose life and love
You, Lord, obey Your voice, and cling to You, for You
are their life and the length of their days. Therefore, my
children are the head and not the tail, and shall be above
only and not beneath. They are blessed when they come
in and when they go out.

I believe and confess that You give Your angels
charge over my children to accompany and defend and
preserve them in all their ways. You, Lord, are their
Refuge and Fortress. You are their Glory and the Lifter
of their heads.

As parents, we will not provoke, irritate, or fret our
children. We will not be hard on them or harass them,
or cause them to become discouraged, sullen, or morose,
or feel inferior and frustrated. We will not break or
wound their spirits, but we will rear them tenderly in
the training, discipline, counsel, and admonition of the
Lord. We will train them in the way they should go, and
when they are old they will not depart from it.

O Lord, my Lord, how excellent (majestic and
glorious) is Your name in all the earth! You have set

Your glory on or above the heavens. Out of the mouth of babes and unweaned infants You have established strength because of Your foes, that You might silence the enemy and the avenger. I sing praise to Your name, O Most High. *The enemy is turned back from my children in the name of Jesus!* They increase in wisdom and in favor with God and man. Amen.

Scripture References

Jeremiah 1:12	Psalm 91:11
Isaiah 54:13	Psalm 91:2
Isaiah 49:25	Psalm 3:3
1 Peter 5:7	Colossians 3:21
2 Timothy 1:12	Ephesians 6:4
Ephesians 6:1-3	Proverbs 22:6
Deuteronomy 30:19,20	Psalm 8:1,2
Deuteronomy 28:13	Psalm 9:2,3
Deuteronomy 28:3,6	Luke 2:52

Child's Future

Father, Your Word declares that children are an inheritance from You and promises peace when they are taught in Your ways. I dedicate _____ to You today, that he/she might be raised as You would desire and will follow the path You would choose. Father, I confess Your Word this day over _____. I thank You that Your Word goes out and will not return unto You void, but will accomplish what it says it will do.

Heavenly Father, I commit myself, as a parent, to train _____ in the way he/she should go, trusting in the promise that he/she will not depart from Your ways, but will grow and prosper in them. I turn the care and burden of raising him/her over to You. I will not provoke my child, but will nurture and love him/her in Your care. I will do as the Word of God commands and teach my child diligently. My child will be upon my heart and mind. Your grace is sufficient to overcome my inabilities as a parent.

My child _____ is obedient and honors both his/her parents, being able to accept the abundant promises of Your Word of long life and prosperity. _____ is a godly child; not ashamed or afraid to honor and keep Your Word. He/She stands convinced that You are the Almighty God. I am thankful that as _____ grows, he/she will remember You and not pass by the opportunity of a relationship with Your Son, Jesus. Your great blessings will be upon _____ for keeping Your ways. I thank You for Your blessings over every area of _____'s life, that You will see to the salvation and obedience of his/her life to Your ways.

Heavenly Father, I thank You now that laborers will be sent into _____'s path, preparing the way for salvation, as it is written in Your Word, through Your Son, Jesus. I am thankful that _____ will recognize the traps of the devil and will be delivered to salvation through the purity of Your Son. You have given _____ the grace and the strength to walk the narrow pathway to Your Kingdom.

I pray that just as Jesus increased in wisdom and stature, You would bless this child with the same wisdom and pour out Your favor and wisdom openly to him/her.

I praise You in advance for _____'s future spouse. Father, Your Word declares that You desire for children to be pure and honorable, waiting upon marriage. I speak blessings to the future union and believe that _____ will be well suited to his/her partner and their household will be in godly order, holding fast to the love of Jesus Christ. Continue to prepare _____ to be the man/woman of God that You desire him/her to be.

_____ shall be diligent and hard-working, never being lazy or undisciplined. Your Word promises great blessing to his/her house and he/she shall always be satisfied and will always increase. Godliness is profitable unto his/her house, and _____ shall receive the promise of life and all that is to come.

Father, thank You for protecting and guiding my child.

In Jesus' name I pray, amen.

Scripture References

Psalm 127:3	Matthew 7:14
Isaiah 54:13	Luke 2:52
Isaiah 55:11	Hebrews 13:4
Proverbs 22:6	1 Thessalonians 4:3
1 Peter 5:7	Ephesians 5:22-25
Ephesians 6:4	2 Timothy 1:13
Deuteronomy 6:7	Proverbs 13:11
2 Corinthians 12:9	Proverbs 20:13
Ephesians 6:1-3	Romans 12:11
2 Timothy 1:12	1 Timothy 4:8
Proverbs 8:17,32	1 John 3:8
Luke 19:10	John 10:10
Matthew 9:38	Matthew 18:18
2 Corinthians 2:11	John 14:13
2 Timothy 2:26	Psalm 91:1,11
Job 22:30	

Prayer for a Teenager

Father, in the name of Jesus, I affirm Your Word
over my son/daughter. I commit _____ to You
and delight myself also in You. I thank You that You
deliver _____ out of rebellion into right relationship with us, his/her parents.

Father, the first commandment with a promise is to
the child who obeys his/her parents in the Lord. You
said that all will be well with him/her and he/she will
live long on the earth. I affirm this promise on behalf of
my child asking You to give _____ an obedient
spirit that he/she may honor (esteem and value as
precious) his/her father and mother.

Father, forgive me for mistakes made out of my
own unresolved hurts or selfishness which may have
caused _____ hurt. I release the anointing that is
upon Jesus to bind up and heal our (parents' and child's)
broken hearts. Give us the ability to understand and
forgive one another as God for Christ's sake has
forgiven us. Thank You for the Holy Spirit Who leads

us into all truth and corrects erroneous perceptions about past or present situations.

Thank You for teaching us to listen to each other and giving _____ an ear that hears admonition for then he/she will be called wise. I affirm that I will speak excellent and princely things and the opening of my lips shall be for right things. Father, I commit to train and teach _____ in the way that he/she is to go and when _____ is old he/she will not depart from sound doctrine and teaching, but will follow it all the days of his/her life. In the name of Jesus, I command rebellion to be far from the heart of my child and confess that he/she is willing and obedient, free to enjoy the reward of Your promises. _____ shall be peaceful bringing peace to others.

Father, according to Your Word we have been given the ministry of reconciliation and I release this ministry and the word of reconciliation into this family situation. I refuse to provoke or irritate or fret my child, I will not be hard on him/her lest he/she becomes discouraged, feeling inferior and frustrated. I will not break his/her spirit in the name of Jesus and by the power of the Holy Spirit. Father, I forgive my child for the wrongs which

he/she has done and thank You that he/she comes to
his/her senses and escapes out of the snare of the enemy
(rebellion). Thank You for watching over Your Word to
perform it, turning and reconciling the heart of the child
to the parents and the hearts of the parents to the child.
Thank You for bringing my child into a healthy relationship with You and with me that our lives might
glorify You! Amen.

Scripture References

Psalm 55:12-14	Proverbs 8:6,7
1 Peter 5:7	Proverbs 22:6
Psalm 37:4	Isaiah 1:19
John 14:6	Isaiah 54:13
Ephesians 6:1-3	2 Corinthians 5:18,19
1 John 1:9	Colossians 3:21
Isaiah 61:1	John 20:23
John 16:13	Ezekial 22:30
Proverbs 15:31	Jeremiah 1:12
Proverbs 13:1	Malachi 4:6

Children at School

Father, in Jesus' name, I confess Your Word this day
concerning my children as they pursue their education
and training at school. You are effectually at work in
them creating within them the power and desire to
please You. They are the head and not the tail, above
and not beneath.

I pray that my children will find favor, good understanding and high esteem in the sight of God and their
teachers and classmates. I ask You to give my children
wisdom and understanding as knowledge is presented to
them in all fields of study and endeavor.

Father, thank You for giving my children an appre-
ciation for education and helping them to understand
that the Source and beginning of all knowledge is You.
They have the appetite of the diligent and they are
abundantly supplied with educational resources, and
their thoughts are those of the steadily diligent which
tend only to achievement. Thank You that they are
growing in wisdom and knowledge. I will not cease to
pray for them, asking that they be filled with the knowledge of Your will bearing fruit in every good work.

Father, I thank You that my children have divine
protection since they dwell in the secret place of the
Most High. My children trust and find their refuge in

You and stand rooted and grounded in Your love. They shall not be led astray by philosophies of men and teaching that is contrary to Truth. You are their shield and buckler protecting them from attacks or threats. Thank You for the angels which You have assigned to them to accompany, defend and preserve them in all their ways of obedience and service. My children are established in Your love which drives all fear out of doors.

I pray that the teachers of my children will be godly men and women of integrity. Give our teachers understanding hearts and wisdom in order that they may walk in the ways of piety and virtue, revering Your holy name. Amen.

Scripture References

Philippians 2:13	Psalm 91:1,2
Deuteronomy 28:1,2,13	Ephesians 4:14
Proverbs 3:4	Psalm 91:3-11
1 Kings 4:29	Ephesians 1:17
Daniel 1:4	Psalm 112:8
Proverbs 1:4,7	Ephesians 3:17
Proverbs 3:13	Matthew 18:18
Proverbs 4:5	James 1:5
Colossians 1:9,10	

The Home

Father, I thank You that You have blessed me with all spiritual blessings in Christ Jesus.

Through skillful and godly wisdom is my house (my life, my home, my family) built, and by understanding it is established on a sound and good foundation. And by knowledge shall the chambers (of its every area) be filled with all precious and pleasant riches — great priceless treasure. The house of the uncompromisingly righteous shall stand. Prosperity and welfare are in my house in the name of Jesus.

My house is securely built. It is founded on a rock — revelation knowledge of Your Word, Father. Jesus is my Cornerstone. Jesus is Lord of my household. Jesus is our Lord — spirit, soul, and body.

Whatever may be our task, we work at it heartily as something done for You, Lord, and not for men. We love each other with the God kind of love, and we dwell in peace. My home is deposited into Your charge, entrusted to Your protection and care.

Father, as for me and my house, we shall serve the Lord in Jesus' name. Hallelujah! Amen.

Scripture References

Ephesians 1:3	Acts 16:31
Proverbs 24:3,4 AMP	Philippians 2:10,11
Proverbs 15:6	Colossians 3:23
Proverbs 12:7 AMP	Colossians 3:14,15
Psalm 112:3	Acts 20:32
Luke 6:48	Joshua 24:15
Acts 4:11	

Complete in Him as a Single

Father, we thank You that _____ desires and earnestly seeks first after the things of Your Kingdom. We thank You that he/she knows that You love him/her and that he/she can trust Your Word.

For in Jesus the whole fullness of Diety (the Godhead) continues to dwell in bodily form — giving complete expression of the Divine Nature, and _____ is in Him and has come to the fullness of life in Christ. He/she is filled with the Godhead — Father, Son, and Holy Spirit — and he/she reaches full spiritual stature. And Christ is the head of all rule and authority — of every angelic principality and power.

So because of Jesus, _____ is complete; Jesus is his/her Lord. He/she comes before You, Father, desiring a born-again Christian mate. We petition that Your will be done in his/her life. Now we enter into that blessed rest by adhering, trusting in, and relying on You, in the name of Jesus. Amen.

Scripture References (AMP)

Colossians 2:9,10   Hebrews 4:10

Part III

PRAYERS FOR CAREERS

Beginning Each Day

Father, as the _____ *(owner, president,
chairman, manager, supervisor)* of _____ *(name of
company),* I come before You rejoicing, for this is the day
which You have made and I will be glad in it. To obey is
better than sacrifice, so I am making a decision to
submit to Your will today that my plans and purposes
may be conducted in a manner that will bring honor
and glory to You. Cause me to be spiritually and
mentally alert in this time of meditation and prayer.

It is into Your keeping that I place my family —
my parents, spouse, children, and grandchildren —
knowing that You are able to keep that which I commit
to You against that day. Thank You for the angels that
You have commanded concerning me and my family to
guard us in all our ways; they will lift us up in their
hands so that we will not strike our foot against a stone.

Thank You, Lord, for the tremendous success that
my associates and I have experienced in our organization and for the increase in profits and productivity we
have enjoyed. Thank You for continuing to influence

every person in this business and every decision that is made. Thank You for Your faithfulness to us day by day and for helping us to become all that You desire us to be.

Thank You, Father, for helping to make us a company that continues to grow and expand. We recognize that without Your help, it would not be possible. Without Your direction and guidance, we would be failures; with it we can prosper and have good success. I continue to thank You for the many blessings that You have poured out upon us all.

I especially thank You for the co-laborers with whom I will be interacting today. Give me words of wisdom, words of grace, that I might encourage them and build them up.

Father, I kneel before You, from Whom Your whole family in heaven and on earth derives its name. I pray that out of Your glorious riches You may strengthen each one with power through Your Spirit in his inner being, so that Christ may dwell in each heart through faith.

Now to Him Who is able to do immeasurably more than all we ask or imagine, according to His power that is at work within us, to Him be the glory in this company and in Christ Jesus throughout all generations, for ever and ever! In Jesus' name I pray. Amen.

Scripture References

Psalm 118:24	Lamentations 3:22,23
1 Samuel 15:22	Joshua 1:8
2 Timothy 1:12	Ephesians 3:14-17 NIV
Psalm 91:11,12 NIV	Ephesians 3:20 NIV

Being Equipped for Success

Father, I thank You that the entrance of Your words gives light. I thank You that Your Word which You speak *(and which I speak)* is alive and full of power [making it active, operative, energizing, and effective].

I thank You, Father, that [You have given me a spirit] of power and of love and of a calm and well-balanced mind and discipline and self-control. I have Your power and ability and sufficiency, for You have qualified me [making me to be fit and worthy and sufficient] as a minister and dispenser of a new covenant [of salvation through Christ].

In the name of Jesus, I walk out of the realm of failure into the arena of success, giving thanks to You, Father, for You have qualified and made me fit to share the portion which is the inheritance of the saints (Your holy people) in the Light.

Father, You have delivered and drawn me to Yourself out of the control and the dominion of darkness *(failure, doubt, and fear)* and have transferred me into the Kingdom of the Son of Your love.

I praise God, the Father of my Lord Jesus Christ, Who has blessed me with every blessing in heaven because I belong to Christ. Your divine power has given me everything I need for life and godliness through my knowledge of Him Who called me by His own glory and goodness. I rejoice in Jesus, Who has come that I might have life and have it more abundantly.

I am a new creation, for I am (ingrafted) in Christ, the Messiah. The old [previous moral and spiritual condition] has passed away. Behold, the fresh and new has come! I forget those things which are behind me and reach forth unto those things which are before me. I am crucified with Christ: nevertheless I live; yet not I, but Christ lives in me: and the life which I now live in the flesh I live by the faith of the Son of God, Who loved me and gave Himself for me.

Father, I attend to Your Word. I consent and submit to Your sayings. Your words shall not depart from my sight; I will keep them in the center of my heart. For they are life *(success)* to me, healing and health to all my flesh. I keep and guard my heart with all vigilance and above all that I guard, for out of it flow the springs of life.

I will not let mercy and kindness and truth forsake me. I bind them about my neck; I write them upon the tablet of my heart. So therefore I will find favor, good understanding, and high esteem in the sight [or judgment] of God and man.

Father, my delight and desire are in Your Law, and on it I habitually meditate (ponder and study) by day and by night. Therefore I am like a tree firmly planted [and tended] by the streams of water, ready to bring forth my fruit in my season; my leaf also shall not fade or wither, and everything I do shall prosper [and come to maturity].

Now thanks be unto God, which always causeth us to triumph in Christ!

In Jesus' name I pray, amen.

Scripture References

Psalm 119:130	2 Corinthians 5:17 AMP
Hebrews 4:12 AMP	Philippians 3:13
2 Timothy 1:7 AMP	Galatians 2:20
2 Corinthians 3:5 AMP	Proverbs 4:20-23 AMP
Colossians 1:12,13 AMP	Proverbs 3:3,4 AMP
Ephesians 1:3 TLB	Psalm 1:2,3 AMP
2 Peter 1:3 NIV	2 Corinthians 2:14
John 10:10 AMP	

Assuring the Success of a Business

Father, I come before You with thanksgiving. You
have qualified and made me fit to share the portion
which is the inheritance of the saints (Your holy people)
in the Light. You have delivered me out of the power of
darkness and translated me into the Kingdom of Your
dear Son.

As I know You better, You will give me, through
Your great power, everything I need for living a truly
good life: You even share Your own glory and Your own
goodness with me! And by that same mighty power You
have given me all the other rich and wonderful blessings
You promised; for instance, the promise to save me from
the lust and rottenness all around me, and to give me
Your own character.

You have delivered me out of the power of darkness
and translated me into the Kingdom of Your dear Son.

Where Your Word is, there is light and understanding. Your Word does not return to You void, but it
always accomplishes what it is sent to do.

I am a joint-heir with Jesus, and as Your son/daugh-
ter, I accept that the communication of my faith is
effectual by the acknowledging of every good thing
which is in me in Christ Jesus.

Father, I commit my works (the plans and cares of my business) to You, trusting them wholly to You. Since You are effectually at work in me [You cause my thoughts to become agreeable with Your will] so that my (business) plans shall be established and succeed.

In the name of Jesus, I submit to every kind of wisdom and understanding (practical insight and prudence) which You have lavished upon me in accordance with the riches and generosity of Your gracious favor.

Father, I affirm that I obey Your Word by making an honest living with my own hands so that I may be able to give to those in need. In Your strength and according to Your grace I provide for myself and my own family.

Thank You, Father, for making all grace (every favor and earthly blessing) come to me in abundance, so that I, having all sufficiency in all things, may abound to every good work.

Father, thank You for the ministering spirits that You have assigned to go forth to minister on my behalf and bring in trade. Jesus said that those who put their faith and trust in Him are the light of the world. In His name my light shall so shine before all men that they may see my good works and glorify You, my Heavenly Father.

Thank You for the grace to remain diligent in seeking knowledge and skill in areas in which I am inexperienced. I ask You for wisdom and the ability to understand righteousness, justice, and fair dealing [in every area and relationship]. I affirm that I am faithful and committed to Your Word. My life and business are founded upon its principles.

Thank You, Father, for the success of my business!

In Jesus' name I pray, amen.

Scripture References

Colossians 1:12 AMP

Colossians 1:13

2 Peter 1:3-5 TLB

Psalm 119:130

Isaiah 55:11

2 Corinthians 6:16,18

Philemon 6

Proverbs 16:3 AMP

Philippians 2:13 AMP

Ephesians 1:7,8 AMP

Ephesians 4:28 AMP

1 Timothy 5:8 AMP

2 Corinthians 9:8 AMP

2 Corinthians 9:8

Hebrews 1:14

Matthew 5:14,16

Proverbs 22:29 AMP

Proverbs 2:9 AMP

Proverbs 4:20-22 AMP

Making a Difficult Decision

Father, I bring this decision before You. It is a difficult one for me to make in the natural, but I know that with You it can be an easy one.

I ask You, Lord, to help me see both sides of this issue and to consider all the facts involved in it. Help me to properly evaluate both the positive and negative attributes of this situation.

Lord, I recognize that an important part of being an excellent manager is decisiveness. In processing the information and considering the possible repercussions or benefits of this decision, help me to avoid the paralysis of analysis. Help me to get the information I need and to evaluate it carefully and wisely.

Help me, Father, to hear Your voice, and so to make the right and correct decision in this case. Keep me from acting in haste but also from delaying too long to reach a decision.

Father, help me not to be influenced by my own personal wants or desires concerning this matter under consideration. Instead, help me to perceive and choose what is best for my department or company, regardless of how I may feel about it personally. Help me to undertake and carry out this decision-making process accurately and objectively.

Thank You for Your guidance and direction in this situation.

In Jesus' name I pray, amen.

Scripture References

Isaiah 11:2 AMP	John 10:27
Colossians 4:1 NIV	Philippians 2:3 NIV
Proverbs 28:1	Judges 6:12

Prayer for the Company

Father, I pray for _____ today. I thank You for this organization and for the opportunity to be a part of it. I am grateful for the chance to earn the income this firm provides for me and my family and for the blessing that it has been to me and all its employees.

Father, I thank You that _____ enjoys a good reputation, that it is seen well in the minds of its customers and vendors. Thank You that it prospers and makes a profit, that You give it favor with its clients, that You continue to provide wisdom and insight to those within it who occupy important decision-making positions.

It is my prayer that _____ will continue to thrive and prosper. Thank You for increased sales and expanded markets.

Thank You, Father, for the creativity that is evident in the different areas of the company — new product ideas and new servicing concepts — innovations and techniques that keep this organization vibrant, alive, and thriving.

I ask You, Lord, to bless it and to cause it to be a blessing to the market it serves, as well as to all those whose lives are invested in it on a daily basis.

In Jesus' name I pray, amen.

Scripture References

1 Timothy 2:1-3	Proverbs 3:21
3 John 2	Psalm 115:14
Joshua 1:8	Proverbs 8:12
Psalm 5:12	Malachi 3:12 AMP
Proverbs 2:7	Hebrews 6:14

Prayer for a Superior

Father, in Your Word, You said to pray for those who exercise authority over us, so I pray for my manager/supervisor today. I ask You to give him/her clarity of thought concerning every decision made this day. Help him/her to clearly identify and accurately assess every potential problem. Help him/her to make the right decisions — to respond, and not to react, to whatever situation or circumstance might arise during the course of the day.

I ask You, Father, to help him/her to set the proper priorities today. Reveal to him/her what tasks are most important and cause him/her to inspire us to perform our duties to the best of our abilities.

I ask that You help him/her to be sensitive to the needs of those under his/her supervision, those who work for him/her. Help him/her to realize that not everyone is the same and that no two people respond or react in the same way. Help him/her to adapt his/her management style or technique to the strengths, weaknesses, and personality type of each individual. Grant him/her the ability to manage beyond his/her own natural gifts and talents. I pray that he/she will rely upon You, drawing strength, wisdom and insight from You.

I purpose in my heart to set a guard over my mouth. I refuse to say anything negative or disrespectful about my manager/supervisor. I choose to support him/her and to say only good things about him/her.

Lord, I ask You to give him/her a peaceful spirit, so that even in the midst of great turmoil he/she may act with surety and confidence and make wise decisions. Help me to be sensitive to his/her needs and responsibilities. Show me ways, Lord, to support him/her and to assist him/her in the performance of his/her duties.

Father, You have said in Your Word that Your Spirit will show us things to come. I ask You to show my manager/supervisor the solution to small problems before they become major problems. Grant him/her creative ideas on how he/she can better lead and manage his/her department.

For all these things I give You thanks, praise and glory, in Jesus' name. Amen.

Scripture References

1 Timothy 2:1-3 AMP   Isaiah 40:29-31 AMP
1 Corinthians 2:16   Philippians 4:7
Ephesians 4:23,24   Hebrews 12:14
Matthew 6:33 AMP   John 14:26
Romans 12:10   John 16:13

Prayer When Persecuted at Work

Father, I come to You in the name that is above all other names — the name of Jesus. Your name is a strong tower that I can run into and be safe when I am persecuted on the job.

Lord, I admit that these unkind words really hurt me. I desire to be accepted by my boss and co-workers, but I long to obey You and follow Your commandments. I know that Jesus was tempted just as I am, but He didn't give in to sin or hate. Please give me Your mercy and grace to deal with this situation. I look to You for my comfort; You are a true Friend at all times.

Thank You, Lord, for never leaving me alone or rejecting me. I make a decision to forgive the people who have spoken unkind words about me. I ask You to work this forgiveness in my heart. I submit to You and reject the disappointment and anger that have attempted to consume me. Specifically right now I forgive _____.

I ask You to cause this situation to accommodate itself for good in my life. **To you, O Lord, I lift up my**

soul; in you I trust, O my God. Do not let me be put to shame, nor let my enemies triumph over me (Ps. 25:1,2 NIV). Because I love You, O Lord, You will rescue me; You will protect me because I acknowledge Your name. I will call upon You, and You will deliver me; You will be with me in trouble, You will deliver me and honor me.

Father, I will resist the temptation to strike back in anger. I purpose to love _____ with the love of Jesus in me. Mercy and truth are written upon the tablets of my heart; therefore, You will cause me to find favor and understanding with my boss and co-workers. Keep me from self-righteousness so that I may walk in Your righteousness. Thank You for sending and giving me friends who will stand by me and teach me how to guard my heart with all diligence.

I declare that in the midst of all these things I am more than a conqueror through Jesus Who loves me. I can use the witty inventions You have provided me, and I will be confident in Your wisdom when working. I am of good courage and pray that freedom of utterance be given to me as I do my job.

In Jesus' name I pray, amen.

Scripture References

Philippians 2:9	Proverbs 3:3,4
Proverbs 18:10	Proverbs 4:23
Hebrews 4:15	Romans 8:37
Proverbs 17:17	Proverbs 8:12
Hebrews 13:5	Psalm 31:24
Proverbs 16:4 AMP	Ephesians 6:19
Psalm 91:14,15 NIV	

Improving Harmony and Cooperation

Devotional Reading

**Fill up and complete my joy by living in
harmony and being of the same mind and one in
purpose, having the same love, being in full accord
and of one harmonious mind and intention.**

Philippians 2:2 AMP

Prayer

Father, Jesus prayed that His followers would be
one. I enter into agreement with my Lord, praying for
the development of harmony and cooperation among
the leadership and employees of Red Lobster *(company
name).* I ask for wisdom to know how to resolve any
conflicts that may have arisen among the departments.

As _____ *(president, supervisor, manager, etc.)*
of _____ I institute the principles of peace,
uprooting and dissolving confusion, rivalries, arguments,
and disagreements for the good of our company
_____ and the welfare of all concerned.

In the name of Jesus I submit myself to You, Father, and resist the devil. I overcome the fear of confrontation (and its outcome) and initiate resolution. I desire to pursue peace with my co-workers, customers, family, and friends.

Give me the courage to go to anyone who is holding anything against me that we might be reconciled. Then I will come and offer my gift to You.

Also, I ask for the boldness of the Lion of Judah to go to anyone who has sinned against me and _____ *(company name),* confronting his/her fault without attacking him/her. I am requesting and believing for reconciliation. Help me to forgive even if he/she refuses to be reconciled and follow through with the necessary steps for his/her good and the company's welfare.

Thank You for the harmony and cooperation necessary to accomplish our common goals.

Glory be to You Who by Your mighty power at work within us is able to do far more than we would ever dare to ask or even dream of — infinitely beyond our highest prayers, desires, thoughts, or hopes. May You be given glory forever and ever through endless ages because of Your master plan of salvation for the Church through Jesus Christ.

In Jesus' name I pray, amen.

Scripture References

John 17:21

James 1:5

James 4:7

Hebrews 12:14 NKJV

Matthew 5:23,24

Matthew 18:15

Ephesians 3:20,21 TLB

Overcoming Negative Work Attitudes

Thank You, Father, for watching over Your Word to perform it as I speak it over myself and those who work with me in Your service, especially _____. I say that he/she is obedient to his/her employers — bosses or supervisors — having respect for them and being eager to please them, in singleness of motive and with all his/her heart, as [service] to Christ [Himself]. Not in the way of eye-service [as if they were watching him/her] but as a servant (employee) of Christ, doing Your will heartily and with his/her whole soul.

_____ readily renders service with goodwill, as to You and not to men. He/she knows that for whatever good he/she does, he/she will receive his/her reward from You.

_____ does all things without grumbling and faultfinding and complaining [against You] and questioning and doubting [within himself/herself]. He/she is blameless and guileless, Your child, without blemish (faultless, unrebukable) in the midst of a crooked and wicked generation [spiritually perverted and perverse], among whom he/she is seen as a bright light (a star or beacon shining out clearly) in the [dark] world.

_____ reveres You, Lord, and his/her work is a sincere expression of his/her devotion to You. Whatever may be his/her task, he/she works at it heartily (from the soul), as something done for You, knowing that [The One Whom] he/she is actually serving [is] the Lord Christ (the Messiah).

In His name I pray, amen.

Scripture References (AMP)

Jeremiah 12:1   Philippians 2:14,15

Ephesians 6:5-8   Colossians 3:22-24

Prayer for an Increase in Personal Productivity

Father, I come to You out of frustration because I am not pleased with my performance on the job. It seems that I am not producing that which I should be producing because I am just not as efficient or effective as I need to be.

Lord, I ask for Your help in planning my day, paying attention to my duties, staying focused on my assignment, establishing priorities in my work, and making steady progress toward my objectives.

Give me insight, Father. Help me to see any habits that I may have that might tend to make me non-productive. Reveal to me ways to better handle the tedious tasks I must perform so that I can achieve the greatest results possible. Help me to organize my efforts, schedule my activities and budget my time.

From books, by Your Spirit, through the people who work with me or by whatever means You choose, Lord, reveal to me that which I need to know and do in order to become a more productive, fruitful worker.

My heart's desire is to give my very best to You and to my employer. When I become frustrated because that is not taking place, help me, Father, by the power of Your Spirit to do whatever is necessary to correct that situation so that I can once again function with accuracy and proficiency.

Thank you, Lord, for bringing all these things to pass in my life.

In Jesus' name I pray, amen.

Scripture References

Psalm 118:24   Psalm 119:99 AMP

Proverbs 16:9 AMP   Proverbs 9:10 AMP

Proverbs 19:21 AMP   1 Corinthians 4:5

Ephesians 1:17

Undertaking a New Project

Lord, I lift up to You this new project which we are considering. I feel that it is one we should be a part of, something we should do, but I seek Your wisdom concerning it.

If it is not of You, Lord, please put a check in our spirits. Direct us to stop planning and working on it and to put a halt to any further waste of time and energy.

If it is of You, Father, then I thank You for Your counsel and assistance concerning it. Give us under-standing and discernment in the preparation stages as we gather the information we need to devise a course of action and to plan the budget for the work. Help us to accumulate the facts and figures we need to carry out this plan in accordance with Your will and purpose.

Thank You, Lord, for Your insight and wisdom. I ask You to give each of us guidance and direction by Your Holy Spirit so we will know how to assimilate the information we gather and use it to maximum advan-tage. Reveal to us any hidden costs or expenses so that we can take them into account in preparing an accurate budget and detailed forecast of both time and money.

Give all of us involved in this project the ability to concentrate our attention and focus our efforts so that we can successfully complete this undertaking and thereby bring honor and glory to You through it.

In Jesus' name I pray, amen.

Scripture References

Proverbs 8:12 AMP

Isaiah 11:2 NIV

Jeremiah 29:11-13

Jeremiah 33:3 NIV

Ephesians 1:8,9,17 AMP

Luke 12:2 NIV

Romans 12:2 NIV

Conducting a Meeting

Father, in the name of Jesus, may Your wisdom prevail today in our meeting. Help each of us to be quick to listen, slow to speak, and slow to become angry, for man's anger does not bring about the righteous life that You desire.

Lord, I recognize Your Holy Spirit and welcome Him to the meeting, acknowledging our dependence upon His presence and guidance. With His help, I purpose to respect and regard every individual's opinions as valuable and worthy of consideration. Knowing that a soft answer turns away wrath, I will be polite and courteous in all our deliberations.

Help each one of us to offer our opinions at the appropriate time and to resist any feelings of self-pity or self-aggrandizement. Guard us from thinking that our opinions are not being heard.

I pray for those who have to deal with rejection. Help them to know that any negation of their opinions or suggestions is not personal.

Should my own opinions be rejected, I refuse to believe that I, personally, am rejected. I will remember that my opinions are not me.

Father, Your love in me does not insist on its own rights or its own way, for it is not self-seeking. I submit to the wisdom that comes from heaven for it is pure, peace loving, considerate, full of mercy and good fruit, impartial, and sincere. As a peacemaker, I sow in peace, reaping a harvest of righteousness.

Thank You, Father, for wisdom that is from above.

In Jesus' name I pray, amen.

Scripture References

Ephesians 1:17	1 Peter 5:5 NIV
James 1:19,20 NIV	Romans 12:10 NIV
John 16:13	1 Corinthians 13:5 AMP
Proverbs 15:1	James 3:17,18 NIV

PART IV

Prayers for Ministry

The Body of Christ

Father, You put all things under the feet of Jesus and gave Him to be head over all things to the Church, which is His Body, the fullness of Him Who fills all in all. We were dead in trespasses and sins, but You made us alive! Christ is our Peace, and we are no longer strangers and foreigners, but fellow citizens with the saints and members of the household of God. Jesus is our Cornerstone.

Father, You want us to grow up, to know the whole truth and tell it in love — like Christ in everything. We take our lead from Christ, Who is the source of everything we do. He keeps us in step with each other. His very breath and blood flow through us, nourishing us so that we will grow up healthy in God, robust in love.

May we be filled with the knowledge of Your will in all wisdom and spiritual understanding. As the elect of God, holy and beloved, we put on tender mercies, kindness, humility, meekness, longsuffering; bearing with one another and forgiving one another. If we have a complaint against another, even as Christ forgave us,

so we also must do. Above all things, we put on love,
which is the bond of perfection, and let the peace of
God rule in our hearts, to which also we were called in
one Body, and we are thankful.

Full of belief, confident that we're presentable inside
and out, we keep a firm grip on the promises that keep
us going. Father, You always keep Your word. Now we
will see how inventive we can be in encouraging love
and helping out, not avoiding worshiping together as
some do, but spurring each other on, especially as we see
the big Day approaching.

Since we are all called to travel on the same road
and in the same direction, we will stay together, both
outwardly and inwardly. We have one Master, one faith,
one baptism, one God and Father of all, Who rules over
all, works through all and is present in all. Everything
we are and think and do is permeated with oneness.

Father, we commit to pray for one another, keeping
our eyes open and keeping each other's spirits up, so
that no one falls behind or drops out. Also, we pray for
our spiritual leaders that they will know what to say and
have the courage to say it at the right time.

We are one in the bond of love, in the name of Jesus.

Scripture References

Ephesians 1:22,23 NKJV

Ephesians 4:15,16 MESSAGE

Ephesians 6:18,19 MESSAGE

Hebrew 10:23-25 MESSAGE

Ephesians 4:4-6 MESSAGE

Colossians 3:12-15 NKJV

Salvation of the Lost

Father, it is written in Your Word, **First of all, then, I admonish and urge that petitions, prayers, intercessions and thanksgivings be offered on behalf of all men** (1 Timothy 2:1 AMP).

Therefore, Father, we bring the lost of the world this day — every man, woman, and child from here to the farthest corner of the earth — before You. As we intercede, we use our faith believing that thousands this day have the opportunity to make Jesus their Lord.

Father, we know that Satan would prevent these from hearing truth, if possible. We are human, but we don't wage war with human plans and methods. We use God's mighty weapons to knock down the devil's strongholds. With these weapons we break down every proud argument that keeps people from knowing God. With these weapons we conquer their rebellious ideas and teach them to obey Christ.

We ask the Lord of the harvest to thrust the perfect laborers across these lives this day to share the good news of the Gospel in a special way so that they will listen and understand it. We believe that they will not be able to resist the wooing of the Holy Spirit, for You, Father, bring them to repentance by Your goodness and love.

We confess that they shall see who have never been told of Jesus. They shall understand who have never heard of Jesus. And they shall come out of the snare of the devil who has held them captive. They shall open their eyes and turn from darkness to light — from the power of Satan to You, God!

In Jesus' name, amen.

Scripture References

1 Timothy 2:1,2 AMP   Romans 2:4

2 Corinthians 10:3-5 NLT   Romans 15:21 AMP

Matthew 9:38   2 Timothy 2:26 AMP

Vision for a Church

Father, in the name of Jesus, we come into Your presence thanking You for _____(name of church). You have called us to be saints in _____(name of city) and around the world. As we lift our voices in one accord, we recognize that You are God, and everything was made by and for You. We call into being those things that be not as though they were.

We thank You that we all speak the same thing: there is no division among us; we are perfectly joined together in the same mind. Grant unto us, Your representatives here, a boldness to speak Your Word which You will confirm with signs following. We thank You that we have workmen in abundance and all manner of cunning people for every manner of work. Each department operates in the excellence of ministry and intercessions. We have in our church the ministry gifts for the edifying of this Body till we all come into the unity of the faith, and the knowledge of the Son of God, unto a mature person. None of our people will be children, tossed to and fro, and carried about with every wind of doctrine. We speak the truth in love.

We are a growing and witnessing body of believers becoming _____(number) strong. We have every need met. Therefore, we meet the needs of people who come — spirit, soul, and body. We ask for the wisdom of God in meeting these needs. Father, we thank You for the ministry facilities that will more than meet the needs of the ministry You have called us to. Our church is prospering financially, and we have more than enough to meet every situation. We have everything we need to carry out Your Great Commission and reach the _____(name of city or country) area for Jesus. We are a people of love as love is shed abroad in our hearts by the Holy Spirit. We thank You that the Word of God is living big in all of us and Jesus is Lord!

We are a supernatural church, composed of supernatural people doing supernatural things, for we are laborers together with God. We thank You for Your presence among us and we lift our hands and praise Your holy name! Amen.

Scripture References

Acts 4:24	Ephesians 4:11-15
Romans 4:17	Philippians 4:19
1 Corinthians 1:10	Romans 5:5
Acts 4:29	1 Corinthians 3:9
Mark 16:20b	Psalm 63:4
Exodus 35:33	

This prayer was written by and used with the permission of T. R. King; Valley Christian Center; Roanoke, Virginia.

Ministers

Father, in the name of Jesus, we pray and confess that the Spirit of the Lord shall rest upon _____ ...the spirit of wisdom and understanding, the spirit of counsel and might, the spirit of knowledge. We pray that as Your Spirit rests upon _____ He will make him/her of quick understanding because You, Lord, have anointed and qualified him/her to preach the Gospel to the meek, the poor, the wealthy, the afflicted. You have sent _____ to bind up and heal the brokenhearted, to proclaim liberty to the physical and spiritual captives, and the opening of the prison and of the eyes to those who are bound.

_____ shall be called the priest of the Lord. People will speak of him/her as a minister of God. He/she shall eat the wealth of the nations.

We pray and believe that no weapon that is formed against _____ shall prosper and that any tongue that rises against him/her in judgment shall be shown to be in the wrong. We pray that You prosper _____ abundantly, Lord — physically, spiritually, and financially.

We confess that _____ holds fast and follows the pattern of wholesome and sound teaching in all faith and love which is for us in Christ Jesus.

_____ guards and keeps with the greatest love the precious and excellently adapted Truth which has been entrusted to him/her by the Holy Spirit Who makes His home in _____.

Lord, we pray and believe that, each and every day, freedom of utterance is given _____, that he/she will open his/her mouth boldly and courageously as he/she ought to do to get the Gospel to the people. Thank You, Lord, for the added strength which comes superhumanly that You have given him/her.

We hereby confess that we shall stand behind _____ and undergird him/her in prayer. We will say only that good thing that will edify _____. We will not allow ourselves to judge him/her, but will continue to intercede for him/her and speak and pray blessings upon him/her in the name of Jesus. Thank You, Jesus, for the answers. Hallelujah! Amen.

Scripture References

Isaiah 11:2,3	2 Timothy 1:13,14 AMP
Isaiah 61:1,6 AMP	Ephesians 6:19,20 AMP
Isaiah 54:17 AMP	1 Peter 3:12

Missionaries

Father, we lift before You those in the Body of
Christ who are out in the field carrying the good news
of the Gospel — not only in this country but also
around the world. We lift those in the Body of Christ
who are suffering persecution — those who are in
prison for their beliefs. Father, we know that You watch
over Your Word to perform it, that Your Word prospers
in the thing for which You sent it. Therefore, we speak
Your Word and establish Your covenant on this earth.
We pray here and others receive the answer there by the
Holy Spirit.

Thank You, Father, for revealing unto Your people
the integrity of Your Word and that they must be firm
in faith against the devil's onset, withstanding him.
Father, You are their light, salvation, refuge, and stronghold. You hide them in Your shelter and set them high
upon a rock. It is Your will that each one prospers, is in
good health, and lives in victory. You set the prisoners
free, feed the hungry, execute justice, rescue, and deliver.

We commission the ministering spirits to go forth
and provide the necessary help for and assistance to
these heirs of salvation. We and they are strong in the
Lord and in the power of Your might, quenching every
dart of the devil in Jesus' name.

Father, we use our faith covering these in the Body
of Christ with Your Word. We say that no weapon
formed against them shall prosper, and any tongue that
rises against them in judgment they shall show to be in
the wrong. This peace, security, and triumph over oppo-
sition is their inheritance as Your children. This is the
righteousness which they obtain from You, Father,
which You impart to them as their justification. They
are far from even the thought of destruction, for they
shall not fear and terror shall not come near them.

Father, You say You will establish them to the end
— keep them steadfast, give them strength, and guarantee their vindication, that is, be their warrant against all
accusation or indictment. They are not anxious beforehand how they shall reply in defense or what they are to
say, for the Holy Spirit teaches them in that very hour
and moment what they ought to say to those in the
outside world, their speech being seasoned with salt.

We commit these our brothers and sisters in the Lord to You, Father, deposited into Your charge, entrusting them to Your protection and care, for You are faithful. You strengthen them and set them on a firm foundation and guard them from the evil one. We join our voices in praise unto You, Most High, that You might silence the enemy and avenger. Praise the Lord! Greater is He Who is in us than he who is in the world!

In His name we pray, amen.

Scripture References

Jeremiah 1:12	Ephesians 6:10,16
Isaiah 55:11	Isaiah 54:14,17
1 Peter 5:9	1 Corinthians 1:8
Psalm 27:1,5	Luke 12:11,12
3 John 2	Colossians 4:6
1 John 5:4,5	Acts 20:32
Psalm 146:7	2 Thessalonians 3:3
Psalm 144:7	Psalm 8:2
Matthew 18:18	1 John 4:4
Hebrews 1:14	

Revival

Father, in the name of Jesus, You have revived us again that Your people may rejoice in You. Thank You for showing us Your mercy and loving-kindness, O Lord, and for granting us Your salvation. You have created in us a clean heart, O God, and renewed a right, persevering and steadfast spirit within us. You have restored unto us the joy of Your salvation, and You are upholding us with a willing spirit. Now we will teach transgressors Your ways, and sinners shall be converted and return to You.

We therefore cleanse our ways by taking heed and keeping watch [on ourselves] according to Your Word [conforming our lives to it]. Since Your [great] promises are ours, we cleanse ourselves from everything that cont-aminates and defiles our bodies and spirits, and bring [our] consecration to completeness in the (reverential) fear of God. With our whole hearts have we sought You, inquiring for You and of You, and yearning for You; O let us not wander or step aside [either in igno-rance or willfully] from Your commandments. Your

Word have we laid up in our hearts, that we might not sin against You.

Jesus, thank You for cleansing us through the Word — the teachings — which You have given us. We delight ourselves in Your statutes; we will not forget Your Word. Deal bountifully with Your servants, that we may live; and we will observe Your Word [hearing, receiving, loving, and obeying it].

Father, in the name of Jesus, we are doers of the Word, and not merely listeners to it. It is You, O Most High, Who has revived and stimulated us according to Your Word! Thank You for turning away our eyes from beholding vanity [idols and idolatry]; and restoring us to vigorous life and health in Your ways. Behold, we long for Your precepts; in Your righteousness give us renewed life. This is our comfort and consolation in our affliction, that Your Word has revived us and given us life.

We strip ourselves of our former natures — put off and discard our old unrenewed selves — which characterized our previous manner of life. We are constantly renewed in the spirit of our minds — having a fresh mental and spiritual attitude; and we put on the new nature (the regenerate self) created in God's image, (Godlike) in true righteousness and holiness. Though our outer man is (progressively) decaying and wasting away, our inner self is being (progressively) renewed day after day. Hallelujah! Amen.

Scripture References (AMP)

Psalm 85:6,7	James 1:22
Psalm 51:10,12,13	Psalm 119:25
Psalm 119:9-11	Psalm 119:37,40,50
2 Corinthians 7:1	Ephesians 4:22-24
John 15:3	2 Corinthians 4:16b
Psalm 119:16,17	

Success of a Conference

Father, we pray that those who hear the messages at the _____ conference will believe — adhere to and trust in and rely on Jesus as the Christ, and that all those You have called to attend the conference will be there and receive what You have for them.

Let it be known and understood by all that it is in the name and through the power and authority of Jesus Christ of Nazareth, and by means of Him that this conference is successful.

Father, Jesus said whatever we bind on earth is bound in heaven, and whatever we loose on earth is loosed in heaven. In His name we bind the will of each person, psalmists, speakers, ushers, and workers to Your will, their minds to the mind of Christ and their emotions to the control of the Holy Spirit. When the people see the boldness and unfettered eloquence of the speakers, they shall marvel and recognize that they have been with Jesus. Everybody shall be praising and glorifying God for what shall be occuring. By the hands of

the ministers, numerous and startling signs and wonders
will be performed among the people.

Father, in the name of Jesus, we thank You that You
have observed the enemy's threats and have granted us,
Your bondservants, full freedom to declare Your message
fearlessly — while You stretch out Your hand to cure
and perform signs and wonders through the authority
and by the power of the name of Your Holy Child and
Servant Jesus.

We thank You, Father, that when we pray, the place
in which we are assembled will be shaken; and we shall
all be filled with the Holy Spirit, and Your people shall
continue to speak the Word of God with freedom and
boldness and courage.

By common consent, we shall all meet together at
the conference. More and more individuals shall join
themselves with us — a crowd of both men and
women. The people shall gather from the north, south,
east, and west, bringing the sick and those troubled with
foul spirits, and they shall all be cured.

I pray for each one participating in this conference.
May every attitude be an expression of the fruit of the

Spirit: love, joy, peace, patience, kindness, goodness, faithfulness, gentleness, and self-control. Lord, I pray that each one will release rivers of living water, an outflowing of the anointing of Your Holy Spirit.

Thank You, Father, for the performace of Your Word in the name of Jesus! Amen

Scripture References (AMP)

Acts 4:10,13,21   Acts 5:12b,13,16

Acts 5:12a   Acts 6:3,10

Acts 4:29-31

Protection and Deliverance of a City

Father, in the name of Jesus, we have received Your power — ability, efficiency, and might — because the Holy Spirit has come upon us; and we are Your witnesses in _____ and to the ends — the very bounds — of the earth.

We fearlessly and confidently and boldly draw near to the throne of grace that we may receive mercy and find grace to help in good time for every need — appropriate help and well-timed help, coming just when we in the city of _____ need it.

Father, thank You for sending forth Your commandments to the earth; Your Word runs very swiftly throughout _____. Your Word continues to grow and spread.

Father, we seek — inquire for, require, and request — the peace of welfare of _____, in which You have caused us to live. We pray to You for the welfare of this city and do our part by getting involved in it. We will not let [false] prophets and diviners who are in our midst deceive us; we pay no attention and attach no significance to our dreams that we dream or to theirs. Destroy [their schemes], O Lord; confuse their tongues for we have seen violence and strife in the city.

Father, You see the regional and cultural strongholds that would hinder the Gospel. You have told us to
declare Your works. So we say boldly that the prince of
the power of the air, the god of this world who blinds
the unbelievers' minds (that they should not discern the
truth), is a defeated foe. We declare on the authority of
Your Word that You have disarmed the powers and
authorities; You made a public spectacle of them,
triumphing over them by the Cross. Thank you, Father,
for the spreading of the Gospel.

Holy Spirit, we ask You to visit our city and open
the eyes of the people, that they may turn from darkness
to light, and from the power of Satan to God, so that
they may thus receive forgiveness and release from their
sins and a place and portion among those who are
consecrated and purified by faith in Jesus.

Father, we pray for deliverance and salvation for
those who are following the course and fashion of this
world — who are under the sway of the tendency of
this present age — following the prince of the power
of the air.

Father, forgive them, for they know not what
they do.

Thank You, Father, for the guardian angels assigned
to this place who war for us in the heavenlies.

In the name of Jesus, we stand victorious over the principalities, powers, rulers of the darkness of this world, and spiritual wickedness in high places over _____.

We ask the Holy Spirit to sweep through the gates of our city and convince the people and bring demonstration to them about sin and about righteousness — uprightness of heart and right standing with God — and about judgment.

Father, You said, **For I know the thoughts and plans that I have for you...thoughts and plans for welfare and peace, and not for evil, to give you hope in your final outcome** (Jer. 29:11 AMP). By the blessing of the influence of the upright and God's favor [because of them] the city of _____ is exalted. Amen.

Scripture References

Acts 1:8 AMP

Hebrews 4:16 AMP

Psalm 147:15 AMP

Acts 12:24 AMP

Jeremiah 29:7,8 AMP

Psalm 55:9 AMP

Acts 26:18 AMP

Ephesians 2:2 AMP

Luke 23:34a AMP

2 Corinthians 4:4 AMP

Ephesians 6:12

Psalm 101:8 AMP

John 16:8 AMP

Jeremiah 29:11 AMP

Proverbs 11:11a AMP

School Systems and Children

Father, we thank You that the entrance of Your
Word brings light and that You watch over Your Word
to perform it. Father, we bring before You the
_____ school system(s) and the men and women
who are in positions of authority within the school
system(s).

We ask You to give them skillful and godly
wisdom, that Your knowledge might be pleasant to
them. Then discretion will watch over them; understanding will keep them and deliver them from the way
of evil and from evil men. We pray that men and
women of integrity, blameless and complete in Your
sight, remain in these positions, but that the wicked be
cut off and the treacherous be rooted out in the name of
Jesus. Father, we thank You for born-again, Spirit-filled
people in these positions.

Father, we bring our children, our young people,
before You. We speak forth Your Word boldly and
confidently, Father, that we and our households are
saved in the name of Jesus. We are redeemed from the

curse of the law, for Jesus was made a curse for us. Our sons and daughters are not given to another people. We enjoy our children, and they shall not go into captivity, in the name of Jesus.

As parents, we train our children in the way they should go, and when they are old they shall not depart from it.

Our children shrink from whatever might offend You, Father, and discredit the name of Christ. They show themselves to be blameless, guileless, innocent, and uncontaminated children of God, without blemish (faultless, unrebukable), in the midst of a crooked and wicked generation, holding out to it and offering to all the Word of Life. Thank You, Father, that You give them knowledge and skill in all learning and wisdom and bring them into favor with those around them.

Father, we pray and intercede that these young people, their parents, and the leaders in the school system(s) separate themselves from contact with contaminating and corrupting influences and cleanse themselves from everything that would contaminate and defile their spirits, souls, and bodies. We confess that

they shun immorality and all sexual looseness — flee
from impurity in thought, word, or deed — and they
live and conduct themselves honorably and becomingly
as in the open light of day. We confess and believe that
they shun youthful lusts and flee from them in the name
of Jesus.

Father, we ask You to commission the ministering
spirits to go forth and police the area, dispelling the
forces of darkness.

Father, we thank You that in Christ all the treasures
of divine wisdom (of comprehensive insight into the
ways and purposes of God) and all the riches of spiritual
knowledge and enlightenment are stored up and lie
hidden for us, and we walk in Him.

We praise You, Father, that we shall see
_____ walking in the ways of piety and virtue,
revering Your name, Father. Those who err in spirit will
come to understanding, and those who murmur discon-
tentedly will accept instruction in the way, Jesus, to Your
will and carry out Your purposes in their lives; for You,
Father, occupy first place in their hearts. We surround
_____ with our faith.

Thank You, Father, that You are the delivering God. Thank You that the good news of the Gospel is published throughout our school system(s). Thank You for intercessors to stand on Your Word and for laborers of the harvest to preach Your Word in Jesus' name. Praise the Lord! Amen.

Scripture References

Psalm 119:130

Jeremiah 1:12

Proverbs 2:10-12 AMP

Proverbs 2:21,22 AMP

Acts 16:31

Galatians 3:13

Deuteronomy 28:32,41

Proverbs 22:6 AMP

Philippians 2:15,16 AMP

Daniel 1:17 amp

Daniel 1:9

1 John 2:16,17 AMP

2 Timothy 2:21 AMP

2 Corinthians 7:1 AMP

1 Corinthians 6:18 AMP

Romans 13:13 AMP

Ephesians 5:4

2 Timothy 2:22

Matthew 18:18

2 Timothy 2:26

Hebrews 1:14

Colossians 2:3 AMP

Isaiah 29:23,24 AMP

American Government

Father, in Jesus' name, we give thanks for the
United States and its government. We hold up in prayer
before You the men and women who are in positions of
authority. We pray and intercede for the president, the
representatives, the senators, the judges of our land, the
policemen and the policewomen, as well as the gover-
nors and mayors, and for all those who are in authority
over us in any way. We pray that the Spirit of the Lord
rests upon them.

We believe that skillful and godly wisdom has
entered into the heart of our president and knowledge is
pleasant to him. Discretion watches over him; understanding keeps him and delivers him from the way of
evil and from evil men.

Father, we ask that You compass the president
about with men and women who make their hearts and
ears attentive to godly counsel and do that which is
right in Your sight. We believe You cause them to be
men and women of integrity who are obedient concerning us that we may lead a quiet and peaceable life in all

godliness and honesty. We pray that the upright shall dwell in our government...that men and women blameless and complete in Your sight, Father, shall remain in these positions of authority; but the wicked shall be cut off from our government and the treacherous shall be rooted out of it.

Your Word declares that **blessed is the nation whose God is the Lord** (Ps. 33:12). We receive Your blessing. Father, You are our refuge and stronghold in times of trouble (high cost, destitution, and desperation). So we declare with our mouths that Your people dwell safely in this land, and we *prosper* abundantly. We are more than conquerors through Christ Jesus!

It is written in Your Word that the heart of the king is in the hand of the Lord, and you turn it whichever way You desire. We believe the heart of our leader is in Your hand and that his decisions are divinely directed of the Lord.

We give thanks unto You that the good news of the Gospel is published in our land. The Word of the Lord prevails and grows mightily in the hearts and lives of the people. We give thanks for this land and the leaders You have given to us, in Jesus' name.

Jesus is Lord over the United States! Amen.

Scripture References

1 Timothy 2:1-3   Deuteronomy 28:10,11

Proverbs 2:10-12,21,22   Romans 8:37 AMP

Psalm 33:12   Proverbs 21:1

Psalm 9:9   Acts 12:24

Members of the Armed Forces

Father, our troops have been sent into _____ as peacekeepers. We petition You, Lord, according to Psalm 91, for the safety of our military personnel.

This is no afternoon athletic contest that our armed forces will walk away from and forget about in a couple of hours. This is for keeps, a life-or-death fight to the finish against the devil and all his angels. We look beyond human instruments of conflict and address the forces and authorities and rulers of darkness and powers in the spiritual world. As children of the Most High God we enforce the triumphant victory of our Lord Jesus Christ.

Our Lord stripped principalities and powers, making a show of them openly. Thank You, Jesus, for defeating the evil one and his forces of darkness for us, and giving us authority to proclaim Your name that is above every name. All power and authority both in heaven and earth belong to You. Righteousness and truth shall prevail, and nations shall come to the light of the Gospel.

We petition heaven to turn our troops into a real peacekeeping force by pouring out the glory of God through our men and women in that part of the world. Use them as instruments of righteousness to defeat the plans of the devil.

Lord, we plead the power of the blood of Jesus, asking You to manifest Your power and glory. We entreat You on behalf of the citizens in these countries on both sides of this conflict. They have experienced pain and heartache; they are victims of the devil's strategies to steal, kill, and destroy. We pray that they will come to know Jesus Who came to give us life, and life more abundantly.

We stand in the gap for the people of the war-torn, devil-overrun land. We expect an overflowing of Your goodness and glory in the lives of those for whom we are praying. May they call upon Your name and be saved.

You, Lord, make known Your salvation; Your righteousness You openly show in the sight of the nations.

Father, provide for and protect the families of our armed forces. Preserve marriages, cause the hearts of the parents to turn toward their children, and the hearts of the children to turn toward the fathers and mothers. We plead the blood of Jesus over our troops and their families. Provide a support system to undergird, uplift, and edify those who have been left to raise children by themselves. Jesus has been made unto these parents wisdom, righteousness, and sanctification. Through Your Holy Spirit, comfort the lonely and strengthen the weary.

Father, we are looking forward to that day when the whole earth shall be filled with the knowledge of the Lord as the waters cover the sea.

In Jesus' name, amen.

Scripture References

Ephesians 6:12 MESSAGE

Colossians 2:15

John 10:10

Ezekiel 22:30

Acts 2:21

Psalm 98:2 AMP

Malachi 4:6

1 Corinthians 1:30

Isaiah 11:9

A portion of this prayer was taken from a letter dated January 22, 1996, written by Kenneth Copeland of Kenneth Copeland Ministries in Fort Worth, Texas, and sent to his partners. Used by permission.

The Nation and People of Israel

Lord, You will not cast off nor spurn Your people, neither will You abandon Your heritage. You have regard for the covenant [You made with Abraham]. Father, remember Your covenant with Abraham, Isaac, and Jacob.

Father, we pray for the peace of Jerusalem. May they prosper who love you [the Holy City]. May peace be within Your walls and prosperity within Your palaces! For our brethren and companions' sake, we will now say, Peace be within you! For the sake of the house of the Lord our God, we will seek, inquire for, and require your good.

Father, we thank You for bringing the people of Israel into unity with each other, and for bringing Your Church (both Jew and Gentile) into oneness — one new man. Thank You for the peace treaties with Israel's former enemies. May these treaties be used for good to make way for the good news of the Gospel as we prepare for the coming of our Messiah.

We intercede for those who have become callously indifferent (blinded, hardened, and made insensible to the Gospel). We pray that they will not fall to their utter spiritual ruin. It was through their false step and transgression that salvation has come to the Gentiles. Now, we ask that the eyes of their understanding be enlightened that they may know the Messiah Who will make Himself known to all of Israel.

We ask You to strengthen the house of Judah and save the house of Joseph. Thank You, Father, for restoring them because You have compassion on them. They will be as though You had not rejected them, for You are the Lord their God, and You will answer them. We thank You for Your great mercy and love to them and to us, in the name of Yeshua, our Messiah.

Father, thank You for saving Israel, and gathering them from the nations, that they may give thanks to Your holy name and glory in Your praise. Praise be to You, Lord, the God of Israel, from everlasting to everlasting. Let all the people say, "Amen!" Praise the Lord.

In Jesus' name, amen.

Scripture References

Psalm 94:14 AMP	Romans 11:7 AMP
Psalm 74:20 AMP	Romans 11:11 AMP
Leviticus 46:22	Ephesians 1:18
Psalm 122:6-9 AMP	Zechariah 10:6,12 NIV
Ephesians 2:14 AMP	Psalm 106:47,48 NIV

Praying the Word
by Germaine Copeland

> **The earnest (heartfelt, continued) prayer of a**
> **righteous man makes tremendous power available**
> **— dynamic in its working.**

> **James 5:16 AMP**

Prayer is fellowshiping with the Father — a vital,
personal contact with God Who is more than enough.
We are to be in constant communion with Him:

> **For the eyes of the Lord are upon the right-**
> **eous — those who are upright and in right stand-**
> **ing with God — and His ears are attentive** (open)
> **to their prayer....**

> **1 Peter 3:12 AMP**

Prayer is not to be a religious form with no power.
It is to be effective and accurate and bring *results*. God
watches over His Word to perform it (Jer. 1:12).

Prayer that brings results must be based on
God's Word.

> **For the Word that God speaks is alive and**
> **full of power — making it active, operative, ener-**
> **gizing and effective; it is sharper than any two-**
> **edged sword, penetrating to the dividing line of**

**the breath of life (soul) and [the immortal] spirit,
and of joints and marrow [that is, of the deepest
parts of our nature] exposing and sifting and
analyzing and judging the very thoughts and
purposes of the heart.**

Hebrews 4:12 AMP

Prayer is this "living" Word in our mouths. Our mouths must speak forth faith, for faith is what pleases God (Heb. 11:6). We hold His Word up to Him in prayer, and our Father sees Himself in His Word.

God's Word is our contact with Him. We put Him in remembrance of His Word (Isa. 43:26) placing a demand on His ability in the name of our Lord Jesus. The woman in Mark 3:25-34 placed a demand on the power of God when she said, "If I can but touch the hem of His garment, I will be healed." By faith she touched His clothes and was healed. We remind Him that He supplies all of our needs according to His riches in glory by Christ Jesus (Phil. 4:19). That Word does not return to Him void — without producing any effect, useless — but it *shall* accomplish that which He pleases and purposes, and it shall prosper in the thing for which He sent it (Isa. 55:11). Hallelujah!

God did *not* leave us without His thoughts and His ways for we have His Word — His bond. God instructs us to call Him, and He will answer and show us great and mighty things (Jer. 33:3). Prayer is to be exciting — not drudgery.

It takes someone to pray. God moves as we pray in faith — believing. He says that His eyes run to and fro throughout the whole earth to show Himself strong in behalf of those whose hearts are blameless toward Him (2 Chron. 16:9). We are blameless (Eph. 1:4). We are His very own children (Eph. 1:5). We are His right-eousness in Christ Jesus (2 Cor. 5:21). He tells us to come boldly to the throne of grace and *obtain* mercy and find grace to help in time of need — appropriate and well-timed help (Heb. 4:16). Praise the Lord!

The prayer armor is for every believer, every member of the Body of Christ, who will put it on and walk in it, for the weapons of our warfare are *not carnal* but mighty through God for the pulling down of the strongholds of the enemy (Satan, the god of this world, and all his demonic forces). Spiritual warfare takes place in prayer (2 Cor. 10:4, Eph. 6:12,18).

There are many different kinds of prayer, such as the prayer of thanksgiving and praise, the prayer of dedication and worship, and the prayer that changes *things* (not God). All prayer involves a time of fellow-shiping with the Father.

In Ephesians 6, we are instructed to take the sword of the Spirit which is the Word of God and **pray at all times — on every occasion, in every season — in the Spirit, with all [manner of] prayer and entreaty** (Eph. 6:18 AMP).

In 1 Timothy 2 we are admonished and urged that **petitions, prayers, intercessions and thanksgivings be offered on behalf of all men** (1 Tim 2:1 AMP). *Prayer is our responsibility.*

Prayer must be the foundation of every Christian endeavor. Any failure is a prayer failure. We are not to be ignorant concerning God's Word. God desires for His people to be successful, to be filled with a full, deep, and clear knowledge of His will (His Word), and to bear fruit in every good work (Col. 1:9-13). We then bring honor and glory to Him (John 15:8). He desires that we know how to pray for **the prayer of the upright is his delight** (Prov. 15:8).

Our Father has not left us helpless. Not only has He given us His Word, but has also given us the Holy

Spirit to help our infirmities when we know not how to pray as we ought (Rom. 8:26). Praise God! Our Father has provided His people with every possible avenue to ensure their complete and total victory in this life in the name of our Lord Jesus (1 John 5:3-5).

We pray to the Father, in the name of Jesus, through the Holy Spirit, according to the Word!

Using God's Word on purpose, specifically, in prayer is one means of prayer, and it is a most effective and accurate means. Jesus said, **The words (truths) that I have been speaking to you are spirit and life** (John 6:63 AMP).

When Jesus faced Satan in the wilderness, He said, "It is written...it is written...it is written." We are to live, be upheld, and sustained by every Word that proceeds from the mouth of God (Matt. 4:4).

James, by the Spirit, admonishes that we do not have, because we do not ask. We ask and receive not, because we ask amiss (James 4:2,3). We must heed that admonishment now for we are to become experts in prayer, rightly dividing the Word of Truth (2 Tim. 2:15).

Using the Word in prayer is *not* taking it out of context, for His Word in us is the key to answered prayer — to prayer that brings results. He is able to do exceeding abundantly above all we ask or think, according to the power that works in us (Eph. 3:20). The power lies within God's Word. It is anointed by the Holy Spirit. The Spirit of God does not lead us apart from the Word, for the Word is of the Spirit of God. We apply that Word personally to ourselves and to others — not adding to or taking from it — in the name of Jesus. We apply the Word to the *now* — to those things, circumstances, and situations facing each of us *now*.

Paul was very specific and definite in his praying. The first chapters of Ephesians, Philippians, Colossians, and 2 Thessalonians are examples of how Paul prayed for believers. There are numerous others. *Search them out.* Paul wrote under the inspiration of the Holy Spirit. We can use these Spirit-given prayers today!

In 2 Corinthians 1:11, 2 Corinthians 9:14, and Philippians 1:4, we see examples of how believers prayed one for another — putting others first in their prayer life with *joy.* Our faith does work by love (Gal. 5:6). We grow spiritually as we reach out to help others — praying for and with them and holding out to them the Word of Life (Phil. 2:16).

Man is a spirit, he has a soul, and he lives in a body
(1 Thess. 5:23). In order to operate successfully, each of
these three parts must be fed properly. The soul or intel-
lect feeds on intellectual food to produce intellectual
strength. The body feeds on physical food to produce
physical strength. The spirit — the heart or inward man
— is the real you, the part that has been reborn in
Christ Jesus. It must feed on spirit food which is God's
Word in order to produce and develop faith. As we feast
upon God's Word, our minds become renewed with His
Word, and we have a fresh mental and spiritual attitude
(Eph. 4:23,24).

Likewise, we are to present our bodies a living
sacrifice, holy, acceptable unto God (Rom. 12:1) and not
let that body dominate us but bring it into subjection to
the spirit man (1 Cor. 9:27). God's Word is healing and
health to all our flesh (Prov. 4:22). Therefore, God's
Word affects each part of us — spirit, soul, and body.
We become vitally united to the Father, to Jesus, and to
the Holy Spirit — one with Them (John 16:13-15,
John 17:21, Col. 2:10).

Purpose to hear, accept, and welcome the Word,
and it will take root within your spirit and save your
soul. Believe the Word, speak the Word and act on the

Word — it is a creative force. The Word is a double-edged sword. Often it places a demand on you to change attitudes and behaviors toward the person for whom you are praying.

Be doers of the Word, and not hearers only, deceiving your own selves (James 1:22). Faith without works or corresponding action is *dead* (James 2:17). Don't be mental assenters — those who agree that the Bible is true but never act on it. *Real faith is acting on God's Word now.* We cannot build faith without practicing the Word. We cannot develop an effective prayer life that is anything but empty words unless God's Word actually has a part in our lives. We are to hold fast to our *confession* of the Word's truthfulness. Our Lord Jesus is the High Priest of our confession (Heb. 3:1), and He is the Guarantee of a better agreement — a more excellent and advantageous covenant (Heb. 7:22).

Prayer does not cause faith to work, but faith causes prayer to work. Therefore, any prayer problem is a lack of knowledge or a problem of doubt — doubting the integrity of the Word and the ability of God to stand behind His promises or the statements of fact in the Word.

We can spend fruitless hours in prayer if our hearts are not prepared beforehand. Preparation of the heart, the spirit, comes from meditation in the Father's Word, meditation on who we are in Christ, what He is to us, and what the Holy Spirit can mean to us as we become God-inside minded. As God told Joshua (Josh. 1:8), as we meditate on the Word day and night and do according to all that is written, then shall we make our way prosperous and have good success. We are to attend to God's Word, submit to His sayings, keep them in the center of our hearts, and put away contrary talk (Prov. 4:20-24).

The Holy Spirit is a divine Helper, and He will direct our prayer and help us pray when we don't know how. When we use God's Word in prayer, this is *not* something we just rush through uttering once, and we are finished. Do *not* be mistaken. There is nothing "magical" nor "manipulative" about it — no set pattern or device in order to satisfy what we want or think out of our flesh. Instead we are holding God's Word before Him. Jesus said for us to ask the Father in His name.

We expect His divine intervention while we choose not to look at the things that are seen but at the things that are

unseen, for the things that are seen are subject to change
(2 Cor. 4:18).

Prayer based upon the Word rises above the senses, contacts the Author of the Word, and sets His spiritual laws into motion. It is not just saying prayers that gets results, but it is spending time with the Father, learning His wisdom, drawing on His strength, being filled with His quietness, and basking in His love that bring results to our prayers. Praise the Lord!

* * *

The prayers in this book are designed to teach and train you in the art of personal confession and intercessory prayer. As you pray them, you will be reinforcing the prayer armor which we have been instructed to put on in Ephesians 6:11. The fabric from which the armor is made is the Word of God. We are to live by every word that proceeds from the mouth of God. We desire the whole counsel of God, because we know it changes us. By receiving that counsel, you will be **...transformed (changed) by the [entire] renewal of your mind — by its new ideals and its new attitude — so that you may prove [for yourselves] what is the good and acceptable and perfect will of God, even the thing which is good**

and acceptable and perfect [in His sight for you]
(Rom. 12:2 AMP).

The prayers of personal confession of the Word of
God for yourself can also be used as intercessory prayers
for others by simply praying them in the third person,
changing the pronouns *I* or *we* to the name of the
person or persons for whom you are interceding and
then adjusting the verbs accordingly. The Holy Spirit is
your Helper. Remember that you cannot control
another's will, but your prayers prepare the way for the
individual to hear truth and understand truth.

The prayers of intercession have blanks in which
you (individually or as a group) are to fill in the spaces
with the name of the person(s) for whom you are
praying. These prayers of intercession can likewise be
made into prayers of personal confession for yourself (or
your group) by inserting your own name(s) and the
proper personal pronouns in the appropriate places.

An often-asked question is: "How many times
should I pray the same prayer?"

The answer is simple: you pray until you know that
the answer is fixed in your heart. After that, you need to
repeat the prayer whenever adverse circumstances or

long delays cause you to be tempted to doubt that your
prayer has been heard and your request granted.

The Word of God is your weapon against the temptation to lose heart and grow weary in your prayer life.
When that Word of promise becomes fixed in your
heart, you will find yourself praising, giving glory to God
for the answer, even when the only evidence you have of
that answer is your own faith. Reaffirming your faith
enforces the triumphant victory of our Lord Jesus Christ.

Another question often asked is: "When we
repeat prayers more than once, aren't we praying
'vain repetitions'?"

Obviously, such people are referring to the admonition of Jesus when He told His disciples: **And when you
pray do not (multiply words, repeating the same ones
over and over, and) heap up phrases as the Gentiles do,
for they think they will be heard for their much speaking** (Matt. 6:7 AMP). Praying the Word of God is not
praying the kind of prayer that the "heathen" pray. You
will note in 1 Kings 18:25-29 the manner of prayer that
was offered to the gods who could not hear. That is not
the way you and I pray. The words that we speak are not
vain, but they are spirit and life, and mighty through
God to the pulling down of strongholds. We have a

God Whose eyes are over the righteous and Whose ears are open to us: when we pray, He hears us.

You are the righteousness of God in Christ Jesus, and your prayers will avail much. They will bring salvation to the sinner, deliverance to the oppressed, healing to the sick, and prosperity to the poor. They will usher in the next move of God on the earth. In addition to affecting outward circumstances and other people, your prayers will also affect you.

In the very process of praying, your life will be changed as you go from faith to faith and from glory to glory.

As a Christian, your first priority is to love the Lord your God with your entire being, and your neighbor as yourself. You are called to be an intercessor, a man or woman of prayer. You are to seek the face of the Lord as you inquire, listen, meditate, and consider in the temple of the Lord.

As one of "God's set-apart ones," the will of Lord for your life is the same as it is for the life of every other true believer: **...seek ye first the kingdom of God, and his righteousness; and all these things shall be added unto you** (Matt. 6:33).

About the Author

Germaine Griffin Copeland, founder and president of Word Ministries, Inc., is the author of the *Prayers That Avail Much* family of books. Her writings provide scriptural prayer instruction to help you pray more effectively for those things that concern you and your family and for other prayer assignments. Her teachings on prayer, the personal growth on the intercessor, emotional healing and related subjects have brought understanding, hope, healing and liberty to the discouraged and emotionally wounded. She is a woman of prayer and praise whose highest form of worship is the study of God's Word. Her greatest desire is to know God.

Word Ministries, Inc. is a prayer and teaching ministry. Germaine believes that God has called her to teach the practical application of the Word of Truth for successful victorious living. After years of searching diligently for truth and trying again and again to come out of depression, she decided that she was a mistake. Out of the depths of despair she called upon the Name of the Lord, and the light of God's presence invaded the room where she was sitting.

It was in that moment that she experienced the warmth of God's love; old things passed away, and she felt brand new. She discovered a motivation for living — life had a purpose. Living in the presence of God she has found unconditional love and acceptance, healing for crippled emotions, contentment that overcomes depression, peace in the midst of adverse circumstances and grace for developing healthy relationships. The ongoing process of transformation evolved into praying for others, and the prayer of intercession became her prayer focus.

Germaine is the daughter of Reverend A. H. "Buck" Griffin and the late Donnis Brock Griffin. She and her husband, Everette, have four children, and their prayer assignments increase as more grandchildren and great grandchildren are born. Germaine and Everette reside in Sandy Springs, a suburb of Atlanta, Georgia.

Word Ministries' offices are located in Historic Roswell, 38 Sloan Street, Roswell, Georgia 30075. Telephone: 770-518-1065.

MISSION STATEMENT
Word Ministries, Inc.

To motivate individuals to spiritual growth

and emotional wholeness,

encouraging them to become more deeply

and intimately acquainted

with the Father God

as they pray prayers that avail much.

You may contact Word Ministries by writing:
Word Ministries, Inc.
38 Sloan Street
Roswell, Georgia 30075
or calling 770-518-1065

www.prayers.org

Please include your testimonies
and praise reports when you write.